DAVID O. McKAY LIBRARY

P9-CJE-685

JUL 15 2003

JUN 17 2024

PROPERTY OF
DAVID O. McKAY LIBRARY
BYU-IDAHO
REXBURG ID 83460-0405

Volume III

HOPE

True Stories of
Answered Prayers

**Edited by
Sophie Elise Lalazarian**

Red Rock Press   New York

Copyright ©2003 by Red Rock Press

ISBN: 0-9669573-9-3

LOC: 2001095474

Published by Red Rock Press

459 Columbus Avenue, Suite 114
New York, New York 10024
U.S.A.
www.RedRockPress.com

This book may not be reproduced, in whole or in part, by any means,
without express written permission by Red Rock Press.

"This New-Old House" by Hugh Howard is reprinted from *The Algonquian.*
Copyright ©2001 by Algonquin Books of Chapel Hill, N.C.

Virtue Victorious angel by Barbara Swanson

Cover Image: Courtesy of Photodisc, ©Photodisc.

Back Cover Art: *Cape Cod Morning,* 1950, by Edward Hopper. National
Museum of American Art, Smithsonian Institution

Cover Design by Kathy Herlihy-Paoli

Book Design by Paul Perlow

I've appreciated the opportunity to work on this project—and I thank Ilene and Richard Barth for believing in me and helping me each step of the way.

My unending appreciation is also due the *Hope* contributors for sharing their stories and for hanging in through the long editing process. This book could not exist without you.

I send a big hug to Peggy Samedi for taking me under her wing and showing me the sights of her hometown, New York. Thank you, also, Ellen Kirshbaum, for your generosity and support.

I am also grateful to my family for their sustaining faith in my potential.

Justin, thank you for putting up with me each and every day, and for your unending love and support, which helps to put everything in perspective.

Thanks be to God, my center and strength.

—Sophie Elise Lalazarian

J. W. Richards

HOPE

TABLE OF CONTENTS

SECTION I

◆ PROMISES OF A NEW LIFE ◆

*"Lord save us all from . . . a hope tree
that has lost the faculty of putting
out blossoms."*
—Mark Twain

GROUND ZERO LIFELINE
Amy Chernoff

The Statue of Liberty gleamed in the brilliant sunshine directly outside our big living-room windows on the morning of September 11, 2001. My husband, Michael, woke with such a tearing backache that he decided, uncharacteristically, to take the day off from work. Nine months pregnant and feeling like a beached whale, I was glad for his company as I struggled with ordinary chores around our downtown Manhattan apartment.

We both excitedly awaited the birth of our first child. Restless, I was calmed by our spectacular Lady-in-the-Harbor view, resplendent in the early morning light. The other side of our apartment building faced squarely west, onto the city, with its office towers and crowded streets, but on my side, I mostly had the calm of the water. I touched my stomach and thought about how soon the baby would arrive, and how my hope of starting a family would within days become a reality.

It was around a quarter to nine when I thought I heard something outside. I didn't think much of it until a friend called, and asked me if I was all right. She said there had been some sort of crash or explosion nearby. Confused, I did as she suggested, and turned on the morning news. A reporter was talking about the twin towers of the World Trade Center. I went to my kitchen, where through a narrow window, I could glimpse the towers.

I saw a huge plume of smoke; one of the buildings seemed to be on fire. I was incredulous, thinking that what was happening was more like a movie than real life. My first reaction was that this could not be possible, and everything would return to normal shortly.

But it didn't stop. It wasn't a movie. This was real.

Downtown New York by John Marin, 1921

I saw the first building crumble and a cloud of debris rush toward me. I screamed and my husband responded by running to the windows to slam them shut as I hurried to the hallway outside our apartment. Would the windows break? We seemed in imminent danger. I yelled to my husband to leave the apartment, and I remember praying for our lives.

After some minutes, we cautiously re-entered our apartment and saw through the windows that the sky had darkened. All was silent. It felt like the end of the world. The sky was so black, like nothing I'd ever seen before. My clock, which said it was only ten a.m., seemed to be lying. Seemingly moments later, the second tower came down. We lost power, and all our communication to the outside world was cut. My husband ran down the 11 flights of stairs to our lobby and then climbed back up again to tell me we needed to evacuate.

I was reluctant to leave. How could I ensure my baby's safety in that outside world? Inside my apartment I felt some measure of control, but once we left the building I didn't know what we could do.

Our lobby was filled with people, bleeding and covered in a heavy white chalk as if they had been dipped in flour. Luckily, a police officer noticed my advanced pregnancy, and quickly escorted my husband and me to a police boat. Our approach to the pier was surreal. The boardwalk, where I'd envisioned pushing my baby's stroller, was destroyed. What was happening? This was not the U.S.A., not with people on the ground clutching blood-soaked bandages, police lining the streets and strange debris filling the air.

Then we were on the crowded police boat to Jersey City— Manhattan in flames behind us. Was this how the beginning of war looked? Or were we witnessing something else? My baby bounced inside me, still secure, but for how long? The boat steamed past the copper lady holding up her lantern. But we and all the other scared passengers were not hopeful immigrants; we were sudden refugees from the heart of the great city. If New York City was a new war zone, what safety could we find across the narrow river?

We arrived at a shelter in Jersey City, and I felt comfort from people who tried to help us. Did we need water or food? Did I need a doctor to examine me? I kept rubbing my belly and telling my baby that everything would be fine, but that she should wait to come out. I did not feel reassured by my own words. My husband made arrangements for us to go to our friend's house in New Jersey. We took every kind of transportation to get there— train, bus, cab and boat, all the while listening to other people's stories of woe.

I felt lucky that I had my husband with me, and that we had

friends who were willing to do anything they could to improve our situation. It occurred to me that Michael might have been maneuvering his car on those tight, crowded downtown streets, and I might have been out walking in search of some last-minute baby thing when everything happened, and I thanked God that we were together and safe. Thousands of other people had not been so fortunate.

That evening, we stayed with a couple that had just had a baby of their own. I cradled their newborn to my body as the four of us sat glued to the TV news. Uncertainty was everywhere—in the world, in our country, and in our own immediate future. What kind of world had I to offer my baby?

Since we'd been evacuated with nothing but the clothes on our backs and whatever we had in our pockets, we had to make do. I could buy a new toothbrush, and wear my friend's maternity clothes for as long as things stayed calm in New Jersey. But the more pressing question was, what of our home?

Michael and I would have—for some weeks or months or maybe for unimaginably longer—no home for our baby, due any day. I could not help but think that when my labor pains came, I'd never be able to reach my hospital on the southern tip of Manhattan, where I'd planned to give birth.

Still, our personal dilemma was overshadowed by the horrors that the TV showed unfolding at our Manhattan doorstep. The area around the building was consumed in fire and agony, where valiant rescuers still struggled against harrowing odds.

Amid my sorrow and anxiety about the attacks, Rachel was born two weeks later at an uptown New York hospital, new to me but safe by some miles from our apartment from which we were still barred. Still, I thought our little family was in the clear, until I learned that she had been born with a serious problem.

Rachel needed an operation to make it possible for her to swallow and digest food. My tiny infant daughter underwent this delicate surgery three days after her birth. We were told that she would have to remain in the hospital for at least two weeks, until she healed and was able to keep food down. During most of that time, neither my husband nor I was allowed to hold her, and we were forced to watch her from behind a pane of glass. I couldn't touch her when I heard cries filled with pain and hunger. I drew on strength I didn't know I had to make it through those weeks. Now, I hold her every chance I get to make up for those horrible days.

We spent the first three months of Rachel's life in a hotel. Normally, I'd have yearned for my personal belongings but the lack of them barely touched me. All of us, but especially little Rachel, had made it through so much already that I was glad we were each in one piece, as New Yorkers struggled to dig out and continued to mourn.

My husband was allowed to return to our apartment for ten minutes to retrieve a few vital possessions. He was given a military escort to our building. That evening he told me that the once-beautiful Battery Park City still resembled a war zone and that army reservists slept in our building, while the park itself had become a command center.

Eventually, we were allowed to return home. As we desperately tried to get back to a somewhat normal life, or as normal as can be living next to Ground Zero, we had another big scare. This one had nothing to do with terror with a capital "T" but everything to do with the fragility of life. We nearly lost Rachel one evening when she suddenly stopped breathing.

We later learned that it's common for children with her condition to choke. The doctor prescribed medication that Rachel would need to take for many months. New feelings of helplessness combined with the memories of the terror I had felt that

September morning; I didn't know how we could keep living so close to all that destruction.

Michael and I thought of moving from Manhattan to the suburbs. Much in our neighborhood remains fraught with grievous image and memory—too much for us, never mind an innocent toddler, to absorb. And there are small, practical concerns. Travel in and from our neighborhood is worse than ever in the 9/11 aftermath, and will be so for years to come. Stores that stock the practical necessities of family life are even fewer and farther than before.

But I can't leave. Looking out onto the water and the Statue of Liberty as I nurse Rachel, I am filled with gratitude and hope. And, even after all is remembered and re-imagined, meditating on this symbol of American promise brings me comfort and peace. This is our home and we will survive what has happened. We stay because this is a place where our little family can grow and flourish. We are nourished each day by the sun streaming in our windows, as well as by little Rachel's grins whenever she notices the beams reflecting in the small waves, the boats bobbing with the tide, and the big-hearted woman of the harbor who seems to smile back at her. Rachel, of course, is still far too young to understand the significance of either the statue or the vast empty pit.

Our apartment house is back to a hundred percent occupancy. Each neighbor who returned to our scarred little part of town has helped me to believe that we can once again have stability and peace.

Rachel is more than double her birth weight and a healthy little girl. We are happy here, and recalling what happened on that fateful day only strengthens my resolve to stay put. I will make this small apartment our home for as long as we can fit into it, buoyed by the love that surrounds me, and the hope embodied by Liberty still standing proudly on the island named after her.

I don't think I realized how powerful my little family could be until little Rachel was born; she made me find the courage to be strong and resilient.

Amy Chernoff and her husband, although raised elsewhere, are proud to be New Yorkers, and thrilled that their baby was born in Manhattan.

PEARLS IN THE SAND

Scott W. B. Grey

My wife sticks a plastic grocery bag into her pocket whenever she heads out onto the beach. We went to the beach a lot more often back when we didn't know if we could have kids. Beachcombing diverts attention from worries. The white noise of the surf washes away stress.

Bev has the biggest sand dollar collection I've ever seen. It was big even before her two-day haul of 113 white discs from a three-mile stretch of Oregon sand. She calls them "gifts from the sea."

Bev says, "I can't leave any of them. If I do, the sea might stop giving them to me." She smiles, but I think she really believes this. So the bag, on every walk. We clamber over rocks, gaze into tide pools, watch the seals, smell the air. Gifts are everywhere.

Through four years of trying, the pills and injections and procedures, and then a miscarriage during one visit to the sea, we learned to take what gifts were offered. The gift in the miscarriage was to learn that a pregnancy was possible.

A ripe follicle in the ovary grows to roughly the size of a grape before it ruptures and ejects the egg growing within. Under the influence of fertility drugs, each ovary can produce more than one egg at a time. My wife's ovaries show up on the fuzzy gray ultrasound screen as a sack of marbles, or a bag of glassy wet stones that glitter in the sun.

On the beach, Bev finds pounds of agates, shiny stones exposed as the rocky areas bordering the beach are eroded. The agate fields shift with the wave action of winter storms, so they are being continually replenished, churned up, recovered, and re-exposed over time.

We've decided that this will be our last try. Neither one of us can stand the thought of another two weeks of blood draws and

injections followed by two weeks of waiting for the disappointment. But this time, she pees on the stick, and it shows two
lines. A year and a half of using every brand of pregnancy test on
the market, and the generic one from the supermarket, tells us
we might have a baby. We remember the miscarriage and that
tempers our enthusiasm.

One day, right in front of our condo, I have to tell Bev to put
back a Lewis Moon Snail the size of a softball. It's still alive. She's
pregnant and doesn't argue. It's turning into a rough pregnancy
and the beach is a good place to be when things are rough. Low
tide and long June days in the sun are the best.

Did I say pounds? One day, I swear, she easily had ten pounds
of agates alone. I shake my head, but I know it makes her happy.
I only have one rule: You carry your own bag.

She touches all her treasures, rearranges them where they
bleach in the sun outside the door of our place at the beach, her
face aglow. Each new outing, she seems to bring home fewer
bobbles than the time before. She's beyond the novelty and now
only looks for those perfect gifts. We're still looking for the agate
the size of my head. We already have one as big as my heart.

This pregnancy is hard. It isn't just the morning sickness, the
moodiness and cravings, the swollen ankles, or the sore back.
Instead, it is all the needles. At first it was the drugs to get pregnant—FSH, HCG, M-O-U-S-E—and then all the shots to try to
stay that way.

The nightly progesterone during the first trimester, in an
attempt to keep the pregnancy viable, is the worst. The sesame
oil suspension has to be injected into Bev's tender bottom with a
large-gauge needle. Unlike saline formulations, the oil isn't
absorbed as quickly, and it spreads the muscle fibers more. It
hurts. Bev can't shoot herself in her own butt, so I'm the one who
has to hurt her every night. Turns out, Bev's allergic to sesame

oil. Each injection site produces a hard lump that quickly becomes inflamed, red and itchy. There's only one pharmacy in all of greater Portland that can mix up the progesterone in a peanut oil base, and it's on the other side of town. During the transition from one form to the other, there is more bleeding. There are more sleepless nights.

We are at the beach when the break-through bleeding happens again. We cry and tell ourselves that it was worth the try, but we try not to call it a miscarriage until a doctor tells us for sure. The next day, after rushing back to Portland, the doctors tell us we haven't lost it yet. So, more progesterone.

There is bleeding nearly every two weeks for those first three months. Every time is agony. And every time, another ultrasound shows us something still growing. "Look!" The doctor extends her hand toward the monitor like a magician. Dots of light flicker on the screen within the image of what appears to be a grain of rice next to a black balloon. "You can see your baby's heart beating." Our own heart rates double, and we smile through tears.

After every scare, the beach is there. The salt air breezes, the knife-edge of sunlight, even the rain and fog are a salve. June at low tide is relief.

Amniocentesis is done with the largest of the needles, easily a foot long. Another ultrasound machine allows a technician to count organs and bones and guide the needle through my wife's abdomen to that perfect position that won't harm the fetus. Two weeks later, we know that our baby girl won't have any of the genetic problems they screened for. We take a deep breath and tell our friends, our families and our co-workers. Their relief is as tangible as our own. The people who work for Bev in one of those monolithic buildings on Intel's Hillsboro campus sigh when they tell her, "We thought you were dying. You were always away at your doctor, and you never told anyone what was happening."

They didn't understand, until that moment, we were dying; we were struggling with life.

The gestational diabetes requires thrice-daily injections that Bev can give herself, sometimes sitting alone in a bathroom stall at Intel. The needles are the smallest of any we've used, but she also has to poke her fingers with a lancet and squeeze drops of her blood onto a test strip several times a day. The tests tell her when to eat more protein or fewer carbohydrates, and how much insulin to inject under the skin of her tummy. More little bottles.

Me, I'm partial to frosted beach glass and the occasional fishing float. My collection is much smaller than Bev's. We're still looking for a Japanese fishing ball. Four inches across, bubbly blue-green glass, a slosh of sea water inside. We know it's out there. They still make them, you know. We look west across the waves, squint into the sunset, and wonder when one will find us.

We are already bored with the weekly visits to the obstetrician by the time we reach "term." The baby isn't due for two more weeks so the doctor surprises us with her grave face. She looks at the seismic squiggles on the graph paper, flowing out of the fetal monitor and says, "I have to confer with one of my colleagues on this." A half hour passes and I'm already late for work when she returns and tells us, "I don't like what I'm seeing on this chart. The baby may be in some distress so, to be on the safe side, I think we're going to deliver this baby today."

The floor gives way from under us again like the deck of a boat pitching down a heavy swell. We're not ready. We fall and fall and fall. Distress is such a simple word and masks so much with its clinical hiss. Our baby is in trouble. The sound of the pounding surf surrounds us, threatens to wash over us; the undertow beckons us out to sea.

❖❖❖

Our daughter's name is Megan; it means pearl. We don't get to the coast for a long time after her arrival. The weather keeps the three of us off the beach the first few times we are able to make it out there. She is five months old before she finally puts her little piggies into the warm sand. Her joy is our joy.

At a year, she walks in the cold water with her little boots and layers and layers of fleecy outerwear. She squeals at the gulls, waddles on the broad wet sands and stares at the crashing waves. The world is new! She flops down on her tummy and churns her arms, an angel in the sand. Her Polartec bunting wicks up the sand with the salt water. It cakes off in the car and makes little drifts and swirls at the bottom of the washing machine.

At 18 months, she knocks down my sand castles and likes to bury her mommy's feet. At two, fistfuls of wet sand are hurled up into the blue sky and she yells "Magic!"

Who can argue?

At three, she can fly a kite. She's a big girl. She'll tell you. Since the moment she could walk, she got her own plastic bag. No shell fragment or broken bit of sand dollar goes uncollected. She's not quite up to a three-mile hike yet, but she delights in her finds as if they were all put there just for her. Some of them are.

And it doesn't take long before she says, "Daddy carry my bag." It's a statement, not a request. I take it from her little hand, like a gift, without a word.

When I put those sand dollars where she can find them, she always pays me back. With change.

Scott W. B. Grey, a software engineer, and his family live in Portland, Oregon.

MY SISTER, JULIE
Melanie Anderson-Caster

My sister Julie is a year younger than I. Born 15 months apart, each on the 15th of the month, we grew up sharing everything: bedroom, clothes, car, phone and friends. Except our dreams. She wanted six kids when she grew up. I wanted to be a writer.

I remember her lying on her bed in the loft we shared, writing lists of potential names for her future children. She'd say them aloud to hear if the first and middle names sounded good together. "Melsie," she'd ask, "how does Ashley Nicole sound? Or what do you think of Trevor Kent?"

"Uh huh," I'd reply, not really listening as I worked on an essay that wasn't due for two more weeks. I don't know why she wasted her time thinking up names for phantom children. She wasn't even old enough to have her period. But all too fast we grew up. After high school, I went away to college; a few years later Julie got married.

Shortly after the nuptials, she was thrilled to learn she was pregnant. An early ultrasound predicted a boy. She quickly named him Patrick Gene and set up a crib.

One morning, only three months into the pregnancy, Julie woke to incredible pain. She saw blood and started throwing up. In her confusion and terror, she didn't realize contractions had started. At the hospital, she stubbornly refused to believe she had lost the baby. She hated that she had no control over her body. "I don't want to lose my baby," she cried.

She underwent surgery to remove the remains of the pregnancy. During surgery, doctors discovered cervical cancer growing rapidly within her body. Doctors quickly performed a "coning" to remove a pie-shaped piece of her cervix. Two weeks later at her follow-up appointment, the surgeon shocked Julie with the news that some of the growth remained. He sent her to see a specialist. "The specialist wants me to have a hysterectomy," Julie told me. Only 22 years old, she was devastated by the news. She pleaded with the doctor to try another surgical coning first: "I don't want to give up my chances of becoming pregnant again. I only care about saving as much of my cervix as possible and having children."

The specialist agreed to try another coning.

Then Julie's marriage began to unravel. She and her husband had yet to celebrate their first anniversary, but it had been a hard year. He had lost his mother shortly before the wedding, and the loss of his unborn child, Julie's cancer and her fierce determination to get pregnant again overwhelmed him. Her husband gone, Julie faced her second surgery alone. The doctors removed another piece of her cervix.

During the next two years Julie remained separated from her husband, but she couldn't bring herself to file for divorce. Depressed, she still longed for a child. Her doctor watched carefully for a return of the cancer. Finally, Julie decided to focus on her broken marriage, and she and her husband reunited. She told me, "We realized that being married and having a family was worth working for, and we decided to get help from an infertility program."

The two spent a private weekend renewing their vows. Julie immediately wanted to get pregnant again. She knew it would be tough. Doctors found endometriosis, a thick lining of scar tissue caused by the two surgical conings. She underwent a painful procedure to remove the scar tissue. Julie and her husband practiced the rhythm method, a regime of temperature taking and following a schedule. She found it difficult to detect her ovulation. "It's all work and no fun," she complained.

Attached by Käthe Kollowitz, 1910

Meanwhile, I had graduated from college, married and was expecting my first child. My pregnancy was a bit of a surprise. It didn't seem fair that it had happened so easily for me while my sister struggled. I avoided talking to her about my joy. We both thought about her miscarriage and the boy named Patrick Gene who should have been the first grandchild in the family.

While I enjoyed a healthy and easy pregnancy with my son, doctors tested Julie's husband and concluded he had "immobile sperm." On top of that, doctors discovered that Julie had lost a gland during the cancer conings; the job of that gland was to help sperm move along. Now, the couple faced "double infertility."

Next, they tried artificial insemination. The stress and pressure of trying to get pregnant took its toll on the marriage. After their fifth attempt at artificial insemination, and two years after they had renewed their vows, they divorced in 1993.

While Julie was waiting for her divorce to be finalized, I discovered I was pregnant again. Another surprise. It took months for me to gather the courage to tell my sister I would soon be the mother of two. I felt guilty that my pregnancies came easily when she so yearned for a child. She'd suffered through a miscarriage, cancer, unsuccessful infertility treatments and a failed marriage. I felt uneasy around her, with a toddler in tow and a belly full of child. I seemed to be living her dream.

"I used to dream of having six kids and living on a farm," Julie acknowledged when I finally shared the news that my second child was en route. "I thought I would get up every morning and feed the animals, then spend the rest of the day taking care of my kids. But now I imagine myself never having kids and I'm resigned to it. I've already grieved, already accepted that I will be childless. I am completely convinced I will never have kids."

In January 1996, Julie found herself in a new relationship and, by that summer, more than eight years after the miscarriage, a miracle happened. She was pregnant. No one was more surprised than she. Though she worried and feared an unhealthy pregnancy, I never saw her happier. But I was afraid to celebrate too soon. I feared if she lost the baby, her spirit might go with it.

Very early in the pregnancy, new challenges arose. Julie's relationship with her boyfriend fell apart and she faced raising her child alone. And there were medical concerns. With an abnormally small cervix, the result of the two coning surgeries, Julie's pregnancy carried high risks. Doctors gave her a slim chance of carrying the baby to full term. Ten weeks into the pregnancy, she experienced blood clotting, cramping, pain and nausea. Thoughts of another miscarriage terrified her. Miraculously, the sonogram showed a strong, healthy baby doing somersaults in her womb.

She entered fulltime bed rest. Doctors performed a procedure that threaded fibers into her cervix to help strengthen it. They warned her that the risky procedure could cause contractions. She spent her bed rest in fear, worrying about having another miscarriage as she lay on the couch. She called me frequently to ask about my kids and to report on her pregnancy. "I'm watching the cobwebs grow and thinking about all the things I could be doing, like cleaning the baseboards. My yard is filling with weeds. Yesterday, I actually got up to do something, but it hurt too much just to bend over. It scared me, so I went back to the couch and stayed there."

Her only trips to the outside world were her doctor's visits twice a month. "It's exciting to leave the house. I see the same road, over and over, the route to the doctor's office, and watch things on that road change. It's my only glimpse of the outside world," she said. "I feel like I'm in prison and that my mind and body are shutting down." Wonderfully, the pregnancy went full term. Ironically, it wasn't easy getting the labor to start. Even though her contractions had begun, she wasn't dilating. She walked, for miles it seemed. Up and down stairs, through hallways, she walked, making the hospital hallways her track. Finally, hospital staff sent her home, but she returned only a few hours later, in a wheelchair, exhausted and in terrible pain. A doctor broke her water to induce labor.

A room full of friends and family joined her for the birth. My dad held the phone near the action so I could hear Julie push her miraculous baby into this world. Christopher Joseph Anderson arrived on April 13, 1997, two days before my 32nd birthday.

But the struggle wasn't over. Christopher had water in his lungs. Hospital personnel assumed he'd swallowed amniotic fluid during the birth and worried about him catching pneumonia. Because of his condition, Christopher went to the Special Care Nursery. Although the hospital planned to release her, Julie managed to stay two extra days. She couldn't go home without her baby. On Christopher's third day in Special Care, the hospital released Julie. A kind nurse set up a cot for Julie in the nurses' lounge, where she slept another night until Christopher stabilized. "It was thrilling on that last night when they unhooked him from everything and wheeled his crib in to stay with me," Julie remembers. "I'll never forget my first time completely alone with him, singing to him and nursing. It was the best night of my life!"

Julie thanks God every day for her blessing. She tells Christopher he is heaven- sent. She wanted six kids. Instead, she says, "I realized that, in the end, my dream still came true. It may not have happened like I expected, but my prayers were answered."

Answered with one precious gift that changed her life. Her miracle baby is now an energetic, enthusiastic, brown-haired, brown-eyed little boy who basks in his mother's love and attention. Julie's life has become what she dreamed of: Halloween trick-or-treating with a pint-size Elvis, karate classes, dinosaur birthday cakes, nighttime lullabies and grocery shopping with a caped crusader. Like his mother, Christopher talks a mile a minute and is passionate about everything. And like the mother she always wanted to be, Julie delights in his every word, feels his every hurt and applauds his every accomplishment. Every wall in her house is filled with pictures of her son. It is a house full of love and gratitude.

As I watch her child and mine grow, I sometimes think of those days long ago when my sister and I lounged on our beds in our shared loft, dreaming our dreams of the future. She never imagined the rocky terrain she would have to travel to realize her deepest wish, and how much sweeter it would be after having trekked the road of pain and persistence. She never dreamed she would struggle so much to have just one child. And in my big dreams of a great writing career, I never imagined I'd write about my sister having a kid.

Melanie Anderson-Caster and her family live in northern California. Ms. Anderson-Caster is a travel writer and contributor to Chocolate for a Woman's Dreams *and* Chocolate for a Woman's Blessings *(Simon & Schuster).*

ROUTES TO PARENTHOOD
Jeanne Ribson

T his really is a tale of four hopes, although it concentrates on my fervent wish that two different children, each having come into this world in bleak circumstances, will have found the loving, consistent nurture each human being needs to blossom. One small embodiment of this wish, at last sight, appeared to be withering—although I pray I'm wrong—and one, I'm confident, is blooming.

After my husband, Michael, and I had two children (our first two hopes) within three years, we knew we'd like another, but not for a while. Our lives were a whirl: two little ones, two full-time jobs, two cars (one of them unreliable) in our suburban driveway. The moment would come, we thought, when there was enough money and time for us to have a third child.

In the blink of an eyelash, our son and daughter had started school, and only the family dog was at home most of the day. When I decided to add a bit of volunteer work to my busy week, I started thinking about babies again.

I became a volunteer who made visits to "boarder babies." These babies were a sad late-1980s and early-1990s phenomenon in New York and other large cities. Abandoned or neglected, but otherwise healthy, these infants lived in hospitals because they had nowhere else to go. Police blamed the crack epidemic that was ravaging inner cities for the increasing number of boarder babies. City social workers said there was a shortage of certified foster homes.

These little ones needed to be held, cuddled, and cooed over. Nurses did their best to pay attention to them, but their first obligation was tending to infants who were ill.

I was assigned a brown-haired, blue-eyed girl with a Spanish last name. Her first name is similar to the one I give her here: "Josie." Josie had spent the better part of her first year in the hospital. When I realized that Josie had no other visitors, I talked to my husband and we decided to become her foster parents. We knew from the start, and explained to our children, that Josie would live with us only until her biological family was able to take care of her. But as time wore on, we began to realize that fact was easy to intellectualize but harder to believe in our hearts.

Josie shared a sunny room with our daughter. It was much bigger than the space foster care rules required, and a world larger than her iron hospital crib. From the moment she entered our home, she was a delight for all of us. I cut back on work hours, our babysitter extended hers, and our children couldn't wait to play with Josie when they came home from school. Josie started to walk (now that she had the space), formed her first words and giggled happily as she explored her new surroundings. Josie was a joy.

The child welfare establishment, however, was no fun. We were servants of a sloppy, sometimes inhumane system which did not respect any of us. We'd receive notices in the mail directing us to report to the city with Josie for a medical checkup or a progress evaluation at a specific time and date, always on a weekday. There was never any negotiation about the time for these appointments. Keeping them meant chucking work for the day and yanking the older children out of school or making complicated alternate arrangements for their pickup and care. Some fiats arrived *after* the stipulated date, earning us foster parent demerits when we failed to appear.

Worst of all, our assigned social worker warned us we were becoming "too attached" to Josie who, she said, should have been placed in a Hispanic foster home. The social worker insisted that Josie was losing the Spanish she'd understood and spoken before she came to live with us. That was absurd. The worker hadn't met Josie in the hospital where she spent nearly her entire first year as a boarder baby. The nurses had spoken to Josie in English as I had. When Josie came to live with us, she hadn't yet begun to talk.

To prove her point, the social worker asked Josie in Spanish how she was, and Josie responded with a giggle. Then I made a *big* mistake. I asked Josie how she was in French, and Josie giggled. The social worker glared at me. I'd questioned her wisdom and thereby doubled her resolve to take Josie from us.

Shortly thereafter, Josie's legal advocate, a diligent young lawyer, who would represent Josie's interests in Family Court, took the time to visit Josie in our home. We learned that Josie's unmarried mother was a woman in her 20s, currently serving a prison term for sale of heroin. There were no siblings or maternal relatives. Whether the woman had left Josie in the hospital to resume her drug-selling career or whether she'd abandoned her there because she knew she was facing a long jail stay was unknown.

Josie's biological father was a man 40 years older than the mother. He possibly lived several hundred miles away, although he collected benefits from the city. The real horror was this: He'd been arrested and charged with sexual molestation of two young girls. The case hadn't gone to trial, probably because there were no adult witnesses to testify.

The advocate told us that the agency responsible for Josie was proposing that her father be awarded custody. She also hinted that Josie's father probably didn't want her and, in any case, there were questions about whether he could provide a decent home.

That night, my husband and I confessed to each other that

What's in a Name?

"TRADITION," as Tevye yelled out in Fiddler on the Roof—national tradition, religious tradition, family tradition.

"What should we name the baby?" is a question that most parents must answer. Poring over baby-name books or thinking about the way a name would sound as you introduced your new arrival—"And this is our baby, Gladys"—leaves some prospective parents anxious and confused. Not to mention the clamor of competing suggestions from relatives. And memory associations: "I knew a girl at school named Abigail and she was a pain . . . " But somehow all babies get named. There are trends, but when all is said and done, more often than not tradition is the winner.

The U.S. Census Bureau reports the most popular baby first names for each year. It probably won't be a surprise to learn that the all-time winner for girls is Mary. In recent years, Victorian-sounding names for girls have made a comeback: Emily and Hannah, for example. But Madison is also a contender.

What about boys? If your child is named John, Michael, Matthew, Jacob, Christopher or Richard, odds are he isn't the only one in your neighborhood.

For Catholics, the names of saints have long been a source of inspiration. The Church once strongly encouraged this. Saints' names are so common in families with Catholic roots that naming a child after a relative often ensures that there's a protective saint hovering in the background.

Names from the Old Testament have become popular recently. You don't have to be Jewish to be called Adam, Noah, David or Jonathan. New Testament names such as Peter and Matthew are male mainstays, even for faiths that eschew saints. Luke is more common now than it once was.

The Bible is also an evergreen source of girls' names. Beyond Mary are Eve, Sharon, Leah, Sarah, Rebecca and Ruth.

Muslim parents often pick names from the Judeo-Christian lexicon, albeit sometimes spelled a bit differently (Ibrahim for

M. Weber

Abraham, for instance) because they also lay claim to that tradition. Of course, multiple forms of Muhammad are invariably popular for boys, along with Omar or Ali. Fatima is an exceedingly worthy girl's name in the Islamic tradition.

Editors of baby-name books usually warn readers to pay attention to initials, pointing out, for instance, that Faith Anne Thomas can boil down to F.A.T.; the name Diane Ursula Mahoney doesn't end up in a happy monogram, either. That bit of advice may sound silly until one recalls how easily some children tease others and how hurtful that may be.

The important message is that a name introduces a person, probably for the rest of his or her life.

we'd be happy to adopt Josie. Each of us had been reluctant to use the "L" word, love, given the tenuous position of foster families. But the notion that a caring biological grandmother or aunt and uncle might show up for our little girl had vanished with the news of her actual prospects. We loved Josie, and we realized our older children considered her part of the family.

I sent Josie's advocate copies of studies of inter-race adoption—they all concluded that it worked out well for "minority" children adopted by "white" families. (I don't consider Hispanics a race but I knew that government characterized children with

Latino surnames as a racial group.) The legal advocate came to agree that we were the best "resource" for Josie, but we were not entitled to speak in Family Court nor have a lawyer speak for us, since Josie had lived with us less than 18 months.

Josie's day in Family Court finally came. Her case was disposed of quickly. We glimpsed Josie's mother in chains; I felt sorry for her but glad Josie did not know who she was. Josie's social work-er appeared with her arm draped over a woman of about 40. This woman was presented as a second cousin of Josie's biological father. The judge speedily agreed with the agency's recommenda-tion that custody of Josie be awarded to her father who, in turn, had agreed to have Josie reside with his cousin.

Because it was almost 5 PM, we were told to bring Josie to the agency at 10 the next morning to relinquish her. The five of us reported to the agency on time, with a vanload of Josie's stuff, and clothes in the next few sizes, too. While we waited three hours for the cousin and the social worker to show up, we played with Josie, hugged her, fed her, talked to her and tried not to cry every time we heard her trilling laugh.

Finally, the cousin and social worker arrived. The father appeared, too, to sign a paper, but hastily said good-bye to his cousin. (Having heard his history, Michael and I both later admitted that we were thinking that it would be a good thing if his disinterest in Josie lasted *forever!*) The cousin, who had very long and pointed bead-studded fingernails, seemed to be avoid-ing her new charge. But before I could worry about those nails scratching Josie, the social worker whisked Josie into the new stroller that we had brought along and wheeled her away, chased by our son and daughter—all three children crying.

We pressed our names and phone number into the cousin's hand, urging her to call us for any information about Josie's habits or any help she'd like.

She never did. When we called her, we found her phone line was disconnected. At Christmas, we sent Josie presents, in care of the agency, but they were never acknowledged. We don't know if Josie received them, or even if she was alive and well.

Our young children were sad for months; my son kept a snapshot of Josie on his bulletin board for years. It hadn't occurred to them they'd never be able to play with Josie again. We were totally cut off from this child we had come to love.

One evening about a year after Josie's departure, Michael said, "Maybe it's time to have another . . ."

I cut him off. Bearing another child wouldn't erase our loss or worry about Josie. Assuring Josie a loving home had been the point. Being a loving family for a child who had no one else had been the point. Michael understood that, too. What he was suggesting was that maybe we should formally adopt a child.

The idea grew on us. Our new hope became a family project. Josie had been a gift. She had made us all realize how much more we had than we required. We had space enough, time enough, and hearts big enough to love someone new. And no child is new for very long.

We'd been too scarred to deal again with any government program, so we turned to a private adoption agency, which helps couples find children, usually from other parts of the world. It took a year, but it was an encouraging and happy experience.

We brought Marianna home from a Kiev orphanage when she was six months old. Thanks to U.S. law reform, she automatically became an American citizen and can even grow up to be president.

The arrival of Marianna didn't obliterate our memories of Josie or our sadness that we do not know how she fares. But both Josie and Marianna have taught us that whatever one has to give to a new child, it's a mere fraction of what that child gives you. Now Michael and I and Marianna's big sister and brother need her every bit as much as she once needed us.

And, except when I write something like this, which glances back at origin, there is *no* distinction in my mind between a biological and an adopted child. Each of my three children has a unique personality and set of talents. Together we are a happy family.

Jeanne Ribson lives in a New York suburb.

THE MATH OF LOVE
Sheila S. Hudson

Melissa was seven weeks pregnant when I received her call. I think we both were in shock as we spoke. I tried to be encouraging; she was troubled. After all, Jonathan her first-born was barely 14 months old. She was a new mother, and I was still learning how to be a perfect grandmother.

It wasn't that I didn't desire other grandchildren, even dream of hordes of them laughing, playing, dribbling, cooing and filling up our retirement condominium with toys, trucks, highchairs and hope. But Melissa's first pregnancy had been achieved only after tests, experimental drugs and artificial insemination. The doctor had warned that only 20% of the time did this treatment result in a viable pregnancy. Melissa had had a difficult nine months, culminating in a Caesarian section to bring Jonathan Hudson Berry into the world. Our prayers had been answered. None of us had dared hope she'd have a second child.

I thanked God for my grandchild every day, and took pleasure in his every gesture, whim, smile and accomplishment. Both sets of grandparents and his aunts and uncles doted on him, the Crown Prince of our family. We dared not ask for more.

But there was more. I grasped for words to express delight, praying that my tone would not betray the fear and worry I felt. Would Melissa carry this baby to term? Would the baby be normal and healthy? And the doubt that most oddly plagued me: If Melissa had a second child, how could I possibly love him as much as I loved the miracle baby, Jonathan?

I hoped I could, but it troubled me greatly that I lacked certainty.

I recalled that when I had been pregnant with my own second child, my husband, Tim, had confessed to similar misgivings. He wondered how he could possibly love another child as much as he loved Melissa. I didn't understand Tim's doubt for I didn't then question that my love could stretch to include any child I was blessed to have. The arrival of Melissa's sister, Jennifer, confirmed the truth of the arithmetic of love, and Tim realized he'd been wrong to worry.

So what was my problem now?

When my daughters had been young, they'd had competitive feelings and had been rivals for the affection of some of our relatives. Perhaps, fearing to see this replayed in a second generation, I found myself hoping for a fair-haired granddaughter—an opposite from her dark-haired big brother, Jonathan. If Melissa had a girl, it would make it easier for me to love her unreservedly, right?

But just before Thanksgiving, we found out that Melissa and David were expecting another baby boy—something to be thankful for, if only the stupid voice inside me would be quiet. Once I had the facts—I was to be the grandmother of two grandsons—I resolved to learn how to play this new role.

When Melissa was 22 weeks into her pregnancy, she and Jonathan were in an automobile accident. Both were taken to the hospital to be checked out. As I awaited test results, I realized not only how much I wanted both Melissa and Jonathan to emerge unscathed, but also how much it meant to me that the child in her belly also be unharmed. I already loved this little-boy-to-be, and with no second thoughts!

The doctor's reassuring report staunched my panic. The threat of losing my second grandson before he was born showed me the obvious. With twinges of shame and guilt, I offered thanks to God for surrounding my loved ones with His guardian angels.

When Melissa was 34 weeks pregnant, she and her husband decided on the name, Andrew David, for their prospective new son. Somehow the fact that he now had a name reinforced my joy at his impending arrival. I eagerly began to chronicle in my journal family events, as Andrew got ready to officially join the family. I looked forward to the day when he was a grown young man and I would hand him these entries to let him know how much he had been loved even before he was born.

On March 10, the 77th birthday of his great grandfather, Andrew was delivered by Caesarean section. He weighed in at a healthy eight pounds—a substantial person from the word go.

Jonathan, at 22 months, might have sensed that his kingdom was threatened, but he also enjoyed the extra attention given him as the big brother. He displayed little self-doubt, only moderate curiosity about the new baby.

As I first held Andrew, my love flowed to him just as it had toward Jonathan. My love didn't double at that moment, it quadrupled.

As Melissa and I locked eyes, I suspected she'd had a few can-I-love-as-much doubts herself, but we never raised that subject between us.

Andrew is now three years old. He has had more than his share of respiratory infections and asthma attacks. Still, he is an affectionate, happy and usually cooperative child. He is also a solo vocalist in a choir only audible to him. His songs are well known in the hospital and doctor's office. I can no more imagine our family without Andrew than I can imagine it without Jonathan. My first grandson taught me even an odds-defying hope may be fulfilled. My second showed me that the mathematics of love is unconditional.

Another brother, Michael, has since joined Andrew and Jonathan, while my youngest daughter, Jennifer, has given birth twice, both times to boys. That makes me grandmother to five energetic preschoolers, each precious one embodying his unique personality and zest for life.

Grandparenting is a challenge that can only be successfully met with humility, the recognition that one can still learn from each new arrival. Grandchildren are gifts who teach us how to expand our love without barriers.

Sheila S. Hudson is the founder of Bright Ideas, a provider of Christian faith-based seminars dealing with inspiration and hope. She and her husband, Tim, live in Athens, Georgia.

SECTION II

◆ MAKING THE VISION REAL ◆

*"Hope ever urges us on, and tells
us tomorrow will be better."*
—TIBULLUS

"MY PAULA"
Paula Gonzalez Ramirez

I lived in Mexico the first four years of my life, and I spoke no English. After my father died, we moved back to the United States with my mother. My older sisters were already in school, and I would watch as they wrote and read. I wanted to be able to read and write, so I would pretend that I was writing, even though it was just doodling. I would get one of my sister's books and get my nose into it and say words just to make believe that I was reading.

I kept telling my mother that I needed to learn how to write. She would write letters of the alphabet, and I would copy what she had written. My mother spoke no English either, but the letters in English and Spanish are the same with a few exceptions. I kept pestering my mother that I needed to learn how to write my name: Maria Paula Gonzalez. In Mexico, the name "Maria" is abbreviated as "Ma." So I learned how to write my name as Ma. Paula Gonzalez.

By the time I entered my first year in elementary school I was anxious to show my teacher that I could write my name even though I could not speak English. When my teacher called out my name, I heard "My Paula." Later, she approached me and said, "My Paula, I want you to take the jump rope out to the playground because it is time for recess."

At seven years old, all I could think about was that my teacher really thought I was special because she kept calling me "My Paula." No other student was getting the special recognition that I was getting. I continued the school year feeling special.

One day, I told my oldest sister that my teacher really liked me because she kept calling me "My Paula."

My sister looked surprised, and explained that instead of writing "Ma," I needed to write "Maria."

"Why?" I asked. Why was my sister contradicting our mother?

My sister explained that the Mexican custom of abbreviating Maria was not familiar to English speakers. And since I was in a U.S. school, I had to follow American spelling rules.

I was embarrassed when I realized that my teacher really didn't think I was special; she just didn't know how to pronounce my name.

I felt I owed my teacher an explanation even though the school year was almost over. I went up to my teacher's desk with my Big Chief tablet and fat pencil that elementary students use. With my thick pencil, I wrote "Ma." and then I wrote "Maria" after it. In faltering English and close to tears, I told my teacher that "Ma." stood for "Maria." My teacher put her arm around me and said, "You will always be 'My Paula' to me even though your name is Maria Paula."

I skipped back to my desk with the relief that only a seven-year-old can understand. My teacher still thought I was special; she loved me. I will never forget Mrs. Dora who taught me how to speak English and at the same time demonstrated that affection overcomes cultural barriers.

Paula Ramirez lives in Austin, Texas, where she is an English as a Second Language instructional supervisor for the Texas Youth Commission.

PANEL TO PANEL
Anthony M. Pearce

"T hey'll rot your mind," barked my father. I stared at the wastebasket in disbelief as a stack of comic books fell into its darkness. How could he do such a thing?

Until that moment, whenever my comics had gone missing, I'd been certain my father had hidden them somewhere: in his closet, in his desk or under his bed. I'd foraged for my comics while my father was away at work and surfaced empty-handed. But that only convinced me I'd not yet found the hiding place; it hadn't occurred to me they were actually gone.

Despite my father—or perhaps because of him—I was, at five years old, certain of three things: My passion for comics would endure. I would learn to write and draw them—indeed even then I tried, with pencil in hand every day until my fingers were chafed raw. And some day I would join the ranks of the professionals.

The stories that danced musically in my mind, that woke me up at night, and entertained me on long lonely afternoons, I would one day share with the world.

The dichotomy that confused me most was that in all other ways my father supported my literacy. He read to me at the dinner table from a collection of illustrated Bible stories and at bedtime until I fell asleep beneath the plaque on my headboard bearing an inscription of the Lord's Prayer. He took me to the library, where I borrowed as many books as I could carry, and hungrily devoured each one. I graduated from *Dr. Suess* to *Encyclopedia Brown* before entering kindergarten. I was bumped from first to second grade based on the highest reading comprehension and retention scores for someone my age that my school had seen. But of all my reading material, comics were my great-

Anthony M. Pearce

est love. My faith in them, in my chosen path, never waned. I only wondered why comic books were so wrong.

I was fascinated with all kinds. Horror comics like "Vault of Terror" and "House of Mystery" kept me glued to their surprise endings. I shared my childhood with Richie Rich's friends, with Archie and the students of Riverdale High. I was enraptured by the majesty of superheroes in their four-color boldness whose morals and values, their codes and inner strengths, became a template, a guide on my path to growing up.

Beyond all else, comics told good stories, with a magical marriage of words and pictures. Because of comic books I was a happy cliché: a little boy with a flashlight, reading under the covers long after bedtime.

Synchronicity smiled on me when I was nine. The Comic-Con International, which attracts tens of thousands of comic book lovers, was born in my home-town, San Diego, California.

Awestruck, I wandered between the rows of dealers' tables, eyes like dinner plates. I passed sections reserved for industry professionals, catching glimpses of creators, deities whose work I worshipped. This was home to me, where I belonged.

Year after year, the convention returned and so did I. After attending several Comic-Cons, and feeling like quite the veteran, I decided it was time to bring my father. It took much persuasion and some out-and-out pleading, but in the end he agreed, and together we entered paradise.

I knew what to expect, but my father did not. He may have thought he'd see things on a par with children's sidewalk chalk scribbles or crayon drawings posted on refrigerators with magnets. Childish things. Foolish games. What he found were art school graduates commanding exorbitant sums for original sketches, editors with literary degrees assigning lucrative jobs to talented hopefuls. And, of course, comics being bought and sold—some for truly impressive prices.

"See that Green Lantern comic?" I asked, pointing. His eyes followed my finger to a clear plastic sheath mounted apart from the others. "The art's by Neal Adams," I explained. "We passed him at the DC booth on the way in. That issue's got an alien that can change colors and he exploits Green Lantern's weakness to anything yellow. It's really cool."

"How do you know that?" my father asked, gawking at the $490 price tag. "It's all wrapped up."

I gazed at him. A long, silent look. "I used to have it," I said.

With five years left until high school graduation, I transferred schools. My new curriculum school focused on graphic arts and I explored any medium offered. Year after year, I was acknowledged as the best artist in my grade, not because my work was exceptional—it wasn't yet—but because the only thing my peers ever saw me do was draw.

Still, I was at odds with teachers who claimed, "any two-year-old could draw comic books." In their eyes, comics were the bastard children of words and pictures, not truly valid in either medium. Art was art. Writing was writing. Comics were neither. Slowly, I withdrew into autodidactic ritual, retreating from the disapproval of those who'd be my mentors only if my aspirations were "higher."

In college art courses, I faced similar obstacles. I embraced the works of artistic masters, but my desire to apply gleaned insights to my own craft was considered blasphemy by my instructors. Frustrated, too close to my baggage to see it, too weighted by the chip I carried, I fled the ivory tower, howling, "Fine! Then show me a two-year-old who can foreshorten in three-point perspective!"

Like actors, singers and astronauts, comic book artists ("pencilers," as they're called in the industry) are just the most visible part of a larger team. But the glamour adhering to pencilers makes for a fiercely competitive field. Recognizing gaps in my education and fearing rejection, I chose a circuitous route to what I hoped would be a successful career. My idea was to launch myself and learn more by working for *Wizard,* the industry news bible of the comic book world. Bluffing my way past a *Wizard* receptionist, I cornered an editor. "How do I write for you?"

And so I began. Article after article, interview after interview, my world broadened. I had lunch with artists, dinner with writers. I drank with editors, and shot pool with publishers. Gradually, my work was published more frequently and my name became known by comic book professionals. Doors opened to me, and soon I was penciling small independent comics, then bigger and better sellers, and finally I was playing with the toys I'd yearned for all my life. It was my turn to tell stories. My turn to draw "Green Lantern."

Anthony M. Pearce

❖❖❖

I hadn't sat in my father's kitchen for some time. It was different, cleaner. The new wife had done good things with it. We sipped a cool soda and stared out at the garden. "Look at *Star Wars*," I spouted. "What Lucas takes millions to achieve, that same story can be told in a comic. Same story, same spaceships and aliens, only it doesn't cost a fortune and the reader is a lot more involved." My father poured himself another soda. "It's the most versatile of all the storytelling mediums," I continued. "You can do anything . . ." My father's look stopped me cold. I felt both foolish and angry.

"Sorry," I resumed. "I just . . . whenever I come into town for the convention I get all worked up again. I'm just so lucky. It's like marrying the woman you love. I courted the business I love and now I get to spend the rest of my life with it." I paused, draining the last of my glass, holding it to my lips long after it was empty. Finally I set it down, and turned back to my father. "But you hate it, don't you?"

We looked at each other for a long time, but neither spoke. "Getting chilly," Dad finally said. "Do me a favor. Grab my jacket from the study, would you?"

I nodded, sliding my chair back and making my way to the study.

"I don't see it," I called to him.

"Have a seat," Dad yelled back, "I'll be right there."

I sat down, fidgeted with a paperweight, and then dropped it back on the desk. Dad entered the room and I looked up. And that's when I saw them. There, decorating the walls, carefully displayed in sheaths of protective plastic, proudly hung in even rows, were copies of every comic or magazine I had ever done.

Anthony M. Pearce lives and writes in San Diego. His comic art portfolio includes pieces for "Crazy-8's," "Predator vs. X," "Green Lantern," "Moon Knight" and "Writer's Bloc."

REPORT FROM A REPORTER
Gina Stewart

I wanted my life to change. I was 12 years old, in eighth grade, and my parents' divorce had just come through. My mother had moved us from Ohio to St. Louis to be with her family and in the hope of finding work. The only one who found steady work was me.

My mother is hearing-impaired; in addition, after ten years of being a stay-at-home mom, her office skills were out of date. As a result, her paychecks were scant. As the oldest child, I did everything I could to make money: baby-sitting, cleaning houses, any and all odd jobs I could find.

I thought of quitting school to work full-time but realized I could not get a "real job" without a high school diploma. School had become just another burden to carry.

In high school, I took a creative writing course because the other choices seemed too difficult. The course held my interest past the first five minutes and, to my amazement, I excelled, receiving several Bs and even an A on a personal essay assignment. I wrote what seemed like a ton of short stories over the first three years of high school, pouring all my pent-up feelings into my pen.

In my final year, I took the school journalism course, which produced the monthly school newspaper. I enjoyed this because we were taught to write only the truth.

As graduation neared, thoughts of going to college for a degree in journalism consumed me, but I feared that my low grade-point average would keep me from getting into a good school. Hope (although it later proved false) came from an unexpected source.

I fell in love with a boy, who offered me marriage, which I eagerly accepted, thinking that this would be a real escape from my joyless life. I figured I could become a waitress or secretary, which would allow me to help out my mother a little each month. I also hoped that these jobs, together with a supportive husband, would give me some free time to try being a freelance writer.

We married when I was 20, and I soon began to fear that I'd traded in one trap for another. I'd found work as a secretary but, even though my husband made good money in advertising, every payday he made me hand over my check, leaving me with a weekly allowance of ten dollars. I didn't like it, but I thought that a good wife should acquiesce to her husband. I told myself that he could only have our best interests at heart.

When my mother understood that I couldn't help out anymore, she acquired some marketable skills by enrolling in beauty school; eventually, she opened her own salon.

Meanwhile, my married situation was deteriorating. My husband kept inexplicably erratic hours. Sometimes he would come home with what I thought was alcohol on his breath, or exhibit wild behavior. I had my suspicions, but I never said anything. I loved him, and tried to whitewash his behavior by reminding myself that he loved me too; wasn't that why we were married?

More than anything, I yearned to be a journalist, full-time, if ever that was possible. Factual reporting seemed more honorable than anything else around me. If I was still biting my tongue when it came to revealing my own troubles, I could write about the world outside me. If I couldn't tell my truth, I wanted to tell someone else's.

I answered an ad in a local bi-weekly paper for a sports section stringer, and got the job. Although it was only part-time (I was still working full-time as a secretary), I realized newspaper reporting was the career for which I was meant. Then one weekend I was assigned to cover a high school baseball game. My husband took the car even though he knew I needed it to get to the game.

> *"We grow great by dreams. All big men are dreamers. They see things in the soft haze of a spring day or in the red fire of a long winter's evening. Some of us let these great dreams die, but others nourish and protect them; nurse them through bad days 'til they bring them to the sunshine and light which comes always to those who sincerely hope that their dreams will come true."* —Woodrow Wilson

I missed the story. My editor told me if it happened again, I would be let go. Of course it happened again, as my husband operated on his timetable alone. I was fired, and devastated.

At 25, I had a baby girl. My connection to her provided the courage to leave my marriage. I couldn't let my little girl grow up with a downtrodden woman as her role model.

It was such a struggle to support my two-year-old daughter and myself on a secretary's income that I needed an extra job. Once again I turned to a bi-weekly newspaper. This time I was hired to write features for a small community paper. I covered school board meetings, store openings, farm shows and everything in between. My daughter often went along on my reporting stints so that we could have time together, and I wouldn't have to spend money on a sitter.

On several occasions, my employer posted ads for full-time reporters. I applied for each and every one, always to receive a letter of "thanks, but no thanks." Finally an editor took me aside and explained that I would not be hired full-time without a college degree.

I immediately enrolled in the local community college and began taking one night course a semester. After a year of juggling working as a secretary during the day, a part-time reporting job and a college course, I took a major new step and applied to be a full-time student at the University of Missouri, which has a very strong journalism program, open only to selected college juniors.

I also applied for financial aid to realize my goal of becoming a full-time undergraduate. My mother called me crazy and my ex-husband sued me for custody of our daughter, then age six. He lost his case and I gained admission to college with financial aid.

My daughter and I moved to Columbia, Missouri, where I began classes in the fall of 1996. Loans and scholarships paid for the bare necessities. School was now exciting because I wanted to be there. I was financially strapped and I still had the pressure of being a single mom but it was endurable because it was my choice. I had a clear focus on what I wanted to accomplish and I was working toward it. It was a joy, many nights, to sit with my daughter at the kitchen table as we each did our homework.

One of my first-year English assignments was to write a personal essay about something that had affected our lives. I wrote an essay entitled "Enough Bad Love" about my marriage and my escape from it. My professor encouraged me to send the essay off to a contest for publication in a book of essays called *Writes of Passage . . . every woman has a story!* The story was accepted, bringing me, I hoped, one step closer to realizing the dream of living by my writing.

At various points during my first two years of college, I added extra part-time jobs to my schedule, but I made new friends, including other single student mothers. I also became the oldest reporter on the school newspaper. Despite my onerous schedule, I pulled B grades. But "B" turned out not to be good enough for the journalism school; I was crushed when I was rejected for that program.

Still, I'd come too far to drop out again. I elected English as my major, which I spiced up with some theatre classes. On graduation eve, I remembered the words of my academic advisor after I'd been rejected for journalism. She'd said, "It's not about which degree program you graduate from. It's what you've learned that's important."

I'd learned many things, but the most important thing wasn't in any of my textbooks. I'd discovered that I am a fighter, and that I could take on the tough stuff in life and learn and grow from it. Proudly, I stepped out into the world with my new degree.

A few months after graduation, I landed a job reporting for a daily newspaper in a town outside of Columbia. Some weeks later, I switched to a lower-paying position on a weekly. The extra time I could spend with my daughter was worth more than the bigger paycheck, and my lean college years had taught me that we could get by financially on less.

I am doing what I so long hoped to do: reporting the facts, telling the truth as best I can, and making a living from it. I am the role model for my 12-year-old daughter that I'd wished to be. I control my own life and that's the best come-true dream of all.

Gina Stewart and her daughter live in Columbia where Gina reports for The Centralia Fireside Guard.

PIGSKIN DREAM
Jodi Benson

Small towns live and die with their sports teams, and my tiny Minnesota hometown was no exception. Peterson was home to fewer than three hundred people, but it was the Tigers' den, and in our pride we bled maroon and gold. During the fall, life had two constants: church on Sunday mornings and football on Friday nights. The minister had our respect, but it was the coach and his 11 disciples who got our blind faith.

My goal, the one that seemed so impossible for a girl to achieve, was to be a real football player. The truth is that the odds were so stacked against this hope that I eventually came near to abandoning it.

As a child, I knew what time of year it was by what sport I was playing. I couldn't have articulated it when I was small, but even then my sense of self-worth was directly proportional to how athletic I was.

The spring of my fifth-grade year, I broke a classmate's glasses and his right forearm when we collided while trying to catch the ratty blue Nerf ball we used in our tackle games. He was eight inches taller and 20 pounds heavier than I. I was on defense, and I thought I had a pretty good shot at an interception until we were both on the ground counting clouds.

When I got up and he didn't, everybody looked at me in disbelief. I felt as if I were Wonder Woman, Batgirl, and She-Ra all rolled into one. It was the first day I knew I wanted nothing other than to play this game forever. The fact that football might not be a viable career choice for a girl hadn't been brought home to me yet.

But my parents, especially my mother, were not long silent on this point. I was a short Korean in an adoptive Nordic family where no one else was under 5'8". My role was of little Jodi, the one who was smart and mature, responsible about her future, goal-oriented and destined for success. In my mom's mind, sports could only be something to keep me fit and in shape, part of an overall package that would emphasize my brain, not brawn.

In the fall of seventh grade, those with the Y chromosome graduated to shoulder pads and helmets. I wanted to be with them, not stuck spiking volleyballs in a stuffy gym. I thought about asking Coach Highum if he'd let me play, and he probably would have said yes, but I knew that when my mother found out she would have started World War III. I stifled my longing to be a gridiron girl in the interest of global peace.

Enviously, I watched junior high boys become men under Friday night lights. I heard about a girl who played wide receiver for a school half an hour away. When we played her team, she never got in the game, and I consoled myself with the thought that that would have probably been my fate too, had I actually been brave enough to go out for the team. Still, I secretly promised myself that some day I'd be an all-star, worthy of all the cheers any bleachers could hold. But the belief that my sport would be football was fading. With each passing month, I felt more removed from the football fantasies born in the stunted grass and hardscrabble dirt of my grade school's playground.

In high school I tried volleyball, basketball, competitive golf and even considered shot-put, but none of them gave me the rough-and-tumble thrill that football had provided. Still looking for something to fill in the gap, I tried fast-pitch softball. They put me in at third base the first year, which I didn't mind, but then I was switched to catcher and found myself at home. The ball wasn't oval but the sonorous thonks of a pitch in my glove and the ponks of my bat were more musical than anything I played on the church organ every other Sunday.

Catcher is a position where hard contact is necessary; I was fear-less. I got stitch marks on my forearms from stopping wild pitches and wore out my shoulder trying to gun down would-be stealers. I was a contact hitter who ran my little legs off while on base. My pri-vate motto was, "I catch therefore I am." My size actually helped me because everybody assumed I was too small to block the plate or take a hit, beliefs I was only too happy to disprove.

One spring day, when it was hot enough to make the air shim-mer, I stood behind home plate in my shin guards and chest pro-tector after the field was raked and chalked, and blissfully absorbed the scent of fresh-cut grass mixed with sweat, leather and dirt. It wasn't football, but I told myself that the feeling was just as good.

Still trying to find that middle ground between my parents' dreams and my own, I decided to apply to Midwestern colleges with good fast-pitch programs, even the Division I schools, and try to make the team as a walk-on. I didn't say anything to any-body for fear that talking about it would make it disappear.

My mother still hoped that sports were just a fad for me, like pre-torn jeans or banana clips. I knew she was ashamed to answer the question, "What's Jodi doing?" with anything close to "She plays ball." Some professions were respectable, some were not, and a daughter who had nearly perfect college-admissions test scores, and still wanted to be a jock was insulting. That sea-son, my parents came to one game but stayed in the car.

After the game, Mom asked me if I couldn't think of a more becoming way to tie my hair back under the catcher's mask, and wasn't it hard on my knees to be going up and down like that all the time? I told her athletes couldn't care less about things like that. Hadn't she seen the way I'd hustled and almost had beat-en a throw to first? I'd advanced the runners, anyway . . .

I was pleased that my mother had been there, but her disap-

FAILURE BEFORE MONUMENTAL SUCCESS

Visit the Lincoln Memorial and you'll gaze on the statue of a great president and heroic orator. But before Abraham Lincoln greatly succeeded, he failed—and more than once. The man behind the icon suffered unemployment and weathered serious bouts of depression. Before he politically triumphed, the electorate rejected him. The log cabin of his earliest years was not only constructed of humble material, it was very small and very crowded, and dark. Lincoln didn't have it easy but he never gave up.

Lincoln began his political career by failing in his bid for the Illinois state legislature in 1832. He tried his hand at being a shopkeeper in New Salem, Illinois, but it just wasn't a good fit. He ran for the legislature again, this time winning his seat. But the death of his sweetheart the following year plunged him into a nervous breakdown. Two years later he ran for Speaker of the House, only to be defeated, and then lost again in 1842 when he ran for Congress.

In 1846, he finally got to Congress but did not win his reelection.

Many of us have heard of Lincoln's rousing performance in the Lincoln-Douglas debates. But although Lincoln was the more stirring speaker, he *lost* the 1858 U.S. Senate race to Stephen A. Douglas. However, his stirring words echoed loudly enough for his party to nominate him for president two years later!

His presidency, of course, got off to the worst possible start when the southern states seceded from the union. As Commander in Chief, Lincoln claimed no laurels for many dark months. The Union Army lost 18 straight battles to Gen. Robert E. Lee's Confederate troops before its first victory.

> We all know of Abe Lincoln's Emancipation Proclamation and we know who won the terrible war. So glorious was his eulogy at Gettysburg, after the battle that turned the tide of the war, that New York's former mayor, Rudy Guiliani, chose to substitute it for any possible words of his own at the Ground Zero one-year commemoration ceremony: *We here highly resolve that these dead shall not have died in vain; that this nation, under God, shall have a new birth of freedom, and that government of the people, by the people, for the people, shall not perish from the earth.*
>
> Lincoln is rightly associated with hope. His failures as well as his successes remind us that hope necessarily has a goal; it points to something better. Hope is the virtue of aspiration and it invariably proceeds from distress with the way things are.

proval hurt, and I continued to look for a way to appease us both.

I decided to take college courses in my senior year of high school. Mom was so excited by my apparent academic dedication that when we visited my future campus she didn't notice I was more interested in the field house than the lecture halls.

My college diamond dreams crashed with my Cutlass Ciera on Highway 16 that fall, leaving me physically intact, though bruised and stiff for about a month, and without transportation to get to practices. I lost my chance to play on my high school team, and my father made me turn in my uniform the day before the playoff game. I entered college, already a failure in my eyes, and ended up flunking in the classroom, too. Deep down, I know now that I was retaliating against my parents' refusal to truly accept what had mattered most to me.

I got married in May 1997, and we moved to North Dakota. I worked as a copy editor at the *Bismarck Tribune*, but soon grew tired of being a pudgy desk jockey. Encouraged by my husband,

I started working out, then joined a women's slow-pitch softball team.

I ended the summer of '98 pitching in a tournament championship game—and I blew it. Worried about failing, every past failure crowded my head and softened my arm. When our coach hoisted the runner-up trophy, I lost it and bolted to an isolated field. There I screamed and cried years of anger and frustration and disappointment into the accepting ground.

When I was done, my teammates handed me Kleenex and Budweiser, unsure of what to do, but behind me all the way.

The next summer, I pitched 37 innings in one day in the Prairie Rose State Games. I played the last eight innings with a broken right pinky on my pitching hand. I'd busted it in the second inning of the fourth game, had gone to the ER to get it fixed, then had returned to the game in the seventh inning and got the last batter to fly out to short right center for the win. I was exhilarated.

My resurrection on the softball field also brought the revitalization of my first hope. Bats and balls were fun but I had never stopped wanting to play football. Then I heard that a women's professional football league was forming in the Twin Cities.

My fingers trembled as I dialed the phone number. Sure, the man said, come on down and show us what you've got. If I had been in the room with him, he would have gotten the biggest, wettest kiss of his existence. It's the least I could have done for someone who had put my lifelong dream within my grasp. But could I really quit my job and throw my life into upheaval for the chance again to chase pigskin?

The answer: Yes! I made the cut, and being a football player has been more fun than illegal fireworks. I've put in three seasons, and I'm in it until I can't play any longer.

The adventure hasn't been trouble-free; my husband got tired of being a "football widow," and now he's my ex. The sport as a whole is struggling financially; with 50-plus teams in as many as eight leagues across the country, travel expenses are high. The lack of organization can make us fractious. However, recent events point to some much-needed unity, and I'm cautiously optimistic for the sport's future.

When I started playing football, I weighed in at almost 175 pounds, with 33 percent body fat. Now I weigh 155 pounds at 19 percent body fat. For a 5'1" woman, that's a lot of muscle, and I'm proud of it. What's more, I now have 50 women who'll back me up in a bar fight, no questions asked. I'm happy, really happy, which is more than most people can say.

I've come to realize that my parents are not bad people. They're just low-risk. I've often wondered if my fearlessness might not come from my mother being afraid enough for both of us.

My mother still wants grandkids, not goalposts. I'm not giving her any choice except to get over it, but I do appreciate how much she cares about me. Dad, while mostly supportive, thinks my sport has no future, and worries about what I'll do next. He may have a point but I don't let it get to me. I've found my silver lining, and it is wrapped around a football.

Jodi Benson is the starting fullback for the Minnesota Vixen, a member of the Women's Professional Football League (WPFL). She encourages young girls to play in the mud and go after their dreams.

LIVE AT FIVE

Steve Seepersaud

I n March of 1997, I was 23 years old and getting ready to graduate from Ohio State University with a masters degree in journalism. I hoped to land a job as a television news reporter. Everything I had heard and read told me the task would be difficult; TV news is a highly competitive field. For every on-air position available, you had about a hundred people who'd give an arm or leg to get the job. My dream was to work my way up the ladder and make it to the network level, to be the next Matt Lauer or Mike Wallace. That was a big mountain to climb. I'd have to land a job at a small station, get a few years of experience, then beat the odds and get a job at a larger station, repeating the process until I reached the network.

An audition tape is a requirement for anyone applying for a job as a TV reporter. It took me several weeks to get one together. I signed out a video camera from our cable access station. Then I went around campus shooting video and doing interviews to put stories together. When I was done, I had news features on tornado safety, the security of information transmitted over the Internet, and a local choral group. It was not exactly the most riveting material and certainly doesn't come close to anything I could do now. I didn't do such a great job shooting video. The pictures were yellow and shaky. In addition, I didn't think I looked all that comfortable on camera, even on my best takes.

I don't even remember how many cover letters, resumes, and audition tapes I sent out. I recall making a few late runs to the post office branch near the Columbus airport. It was open 24 hours a day; I'd sometimes mail packages late at night because I couldn't stand seeing them in my apartment any longer.

A few weeks after mailing the application material, I hoped to get calls from news directors inviting me to interviews. Not one person called. I was still determined to do whatever I could to get my foot in the door. So I got on the phone to invite myself to television stations in New York, Pennsylvania, Ohio and West Virginia.

I passed a whole week on the telephone. I spent about $50 on long distance calls, talking to dozens of people, leaving voice mails and being tossed back and forth from newsrooms to switchboard operators. When it was all said and done, I had lined up two meetings with news directors. They didn't have any jobs open, but I wasn't worried. I figured that if the meetings went well, they'd remember me when a position did become available.

The first interview was at the NBC station in Parkersburg, West Virginia. To me, it seemed to go pretty well. It helped that the news director was an Ohio State alum. She said that my tape was "not bad," and that I showed potential. Before I left, she told me to stay in touch. My next stop was the ABC station in Elmira, New York. The interview did not go smoothly at all. The news director had some trouble locating my audition tape. When it was found, I discovered it had been damaged in the mail. When we tried to play it, there were tracking lines that we could not get rid of. He didn't seem the least bit thrilled with my work, but offered suggestions as we viewed the tape. His overall opinion was that I was most likely not going to find a job in the business.

His conclusion played over and over in my head. It was hard to shrug off, that he didn't think I would ever get a job. He'd voiced my biggest fear.

Comforting myself with statements taken from employment guides, I reminded myself of what I'd read. Pronouncements such as "What one news director dislikes, another admires," and

"You cannot be all things to all people," helped me to shake off the news director's comment.

I decided to work on improving my tape, using some of the suggestions that I'd picked up on my road trip. I figured that my goal was to get the best possible tape in front of the right person. Ever hopeful, I also applied for producer positions in the hope that I could slide into an on-air gig.

A few weeks later, I interviewed at the NBC station in Lima, Ohio. This time, a reporter job was open. My conversation with the news director went very well. I felt confident that I'd be hired. I waited for him to call me back. Days went by and nothing happened. I finally called him, only to learn that another candidate had accepted the job. I was very disappointed. I felt angry at myself and at the world. I thought that I'd had a shot at that job. Now I wondered if I'd ever get a chance to live my dream.

But as time passed, my anger turned into determination. I was not going to let anything get in the way of getting a job in the TV news business. I was going to show the man in Elmira and the other news directors that they were wrong about me. I figured I would be like one of those athletes who were told they'd never make it, but who went on to become stars.

Even though Lima is a small town, it had another TV news outfit. I sent a tape there in early July, and called a few weeks later to follow up. A reporter job was open at an independent Christian station, and the news director, Stuart Hall, told me he'd be glad to have me in for a meeting. It could not have gone better. After giving me a tour of the station, Stuart chatted with me for about an hour. I wasn't too surprised when I was called back for a second interview. This time, I had to meet with the station's program manager. That meeting seemed to go pretty well except for the fact that I felt he had a problem with my education. He seemed to have a look of disdain on his face when I

> *"What happens to a dream deferred? Does it dry up like a raisin in the sun? . . . Or does it explode?"*
> —Langston Hughes

told him I had a master's degree. He emphasized real world experience and brought up the fact that he had succeeded without attending college. I worried that my graduate degree would be a liability instead of an asset.

I was told that they'd call me with a decision a few days later. Time passed but I didn't hear anything. I called up the program director and he said they still needed a few more days. I really wanted that job. After months of searching, I felt that I was really close to landing something. I didn't even want to think about what I would do if they gave the job to someone else.

I didn't have to think about it. Four days later they called me, offering the job. That ended six months of job searching; I could finally quit work as a supermarket cashier.

For the next few months, I had an absolute blast in Lima. After starting out as a news reporter, I got to try my hand at sportscasts. I covered a few Ohio State football games. And I was promoted to the morning anchor/producer slot. I had to wake with the chickens, but the extra airtime and experience made it worthwhile. It was great seeing myself on television, and showing off my new tape to proud family members and friends.

It all ended a few months later. The station managers had decided that running a news department was too much trouble and expense. So my co-workers and I were out of jobs. Luckily for me, I had signed a contract. The buyout gave me money to live on while I looked for another job.

The next few months were rough. The self-doubts from the first job search came flooding back. It seemed as if the odds were very much against me. But I knew I had overcome this before, and I thought I could do it again. It only took three months for me to be proved correct. I landed a job at a station in Binghamton, New York. Binghamton was a bigger media market and I'd be making better money. On top of that, I'd be living closer to my parents, who live on Long Island.

I've now spent a few years in Binghamton. I started as a reporter/photographer and have worked myself upward into a management position. I've had the chance to learn a lot about the business, improve my skills and work with some great people.

When I think about my career, I see that some of my initial hopes were unrealistic. When I was in school, I felt that I had to be a network-level anchor to be successful in the business. Now I realize that there is much success to be enjoyed outside of the "majors." Not every talented young baseball player can be a star like Reggie Jackson or Mark McGwire. Not every solid newsman gets to the networks. But even though I'm not seen coast to coast, I believe I'm doing good work. I've become a T.V. pro.

I've also learned how important it is to believe in your own abilities and to stick by the belief that you'll succeed. That helped me to get through those rough times when I was looking for work in the business. Hope also helped me after I had landed the job, during those dark times when I'd have self-doubt and worry that my career wasn't going anywhere.

Steve Seepersaud is the assignment editor of the ABC affiliate in Binghamton, New York. In 2000, the New York State Associated Press awarded him first prize in the category of best interview.

IT'S NEVER TOO LATE
Judith Z. Marrs

Blood seeped through stubborn cracks in my crinkled hands. Huge globs of petroleum jelly could not stop the blood from dripping onto the metal kitchen sink. My nightly ritual of coating my sore fingers with Vaseline and applying gloves, coupled with my prayers to Jesus, Joseph, Mary, St. Anthony and St. Theresa, was not being honored with the healing I desired. But I continued to scour hard crust off the pans that an hour of soaking in blue dishwashing detergent wouldn't loosen. I racked my brain for a better way to supplement my husband's salary as a road musician than working at my folks' hamburger hangout for the local yokels.

It was the winter of 1982, in a small town in northern Mississippi, when I tended to my chapped hands. It was off-season for road musicians, and we had five young children who had grown fond of luxuries like food, warmth and clothing. One would think that playing drums and being a road manager/ bus driver for country music stars would provide a decent income. But, no, that's just a young man's fairytale. My husband loves music and has this gift for it. He has played for presidents at the White House, has been on USO tours, and has appeared on almost every major television network. Successful though he might have seemed, like most supporting musicians he was underpaid. Headliners make big bucks and can afford to take off for months at a time, leaving the backup musicians to gig in clubs for little or nothing. My husband wasn't a headliner, and I was forced to work at my father's cafe, washing dishes, waiting on customers and flipping burgers while simultaneously juggling the care of my numerous kids.

On that trying day, I took a long hard look at my bloodied

hands and realized that I'd spend the rest of my life painfully scrubbing stubborn pans if I didn't alter course soon. Before I could change my mind, I quickly threw my dishrag in the sink and announced, "I'm going to college." Just like that. I wasn't thinking: Should I do this? I knew that I had to.

Papa Joe had a far from positive reaction. He *needed* me at the café, he insisted. And I would eventually be happy I'd stayed: "This will all be yours some day. Don't quit."

I'd heard it before. But this time I didn't stay put. I wanted a change. Connie, a waitress at Papa Joe's, was in nursing school, and she'd told me the going hourly rate for nurses at local hospitals. My heart grew greedy. Although I'd always had a desire to teach school, I knew that Mississippi teachers were nearly the lowest paid in the nation. So I decided I would become a rich nurse instead.

I walked out the door, got into my car and drove straight to Northwest Community College. I applied for a government Pell Grant that would cover tuition and textbooks. And I got it! Sometimes it pays to be both poor and determined.

Enrollment was scary but my first class in Anatomy and Physiology was even more frightening. Sitting in class, just glancing around at the younger students, made me anxious. *Oh my Lord. What was I thinking? I can never do this,* I thought to myself as I thumbed through the textbook. It had been many years and five babies since I had sat at a classroom desk. I was 36, and I was afraid that was too old to be a successful college student. Fear made it hard to concentrate. I thought my brain was too clogged down with nonintellectual babble to comprehend anything about the body systems and how they worked. I expressed my anxiety to the 18-year-old child sitting next to me: "Ha! I can never learn all this."

She looked back at me and said, "Sure you can."

She told me to use bright yellow marker when I studied; she swore highlighted passages embedded themselves in the brain. While highlighting was helpful, I needed to take more extreme measures. Returning from class every night I would sit down and recopy my notes until I remembered them word for word. Sometimes it took all night.

During the four years it took to become a registered nurse, I learned how to study at unusual places—my children's soccer practices, in the waiting room of a dentist's office—and while jiggling a child on one hip at two in the morning. One thing no nursing instructor taught me is why all earaches begin to arc upwards at 2 AM

Soon after I started the clinical part of my training, the hands-on part, where we faced real patients, my mother was diagnosed with a malignant brain tumor. Most nights of her illness I spent by her side. Before her surgery, she proudly told her nurses that I would soon join their ranks. My mom did not beat the odds, and soon she was comatose. I rendered her what small mercies I could between bouts of studying on a cot by her bedside.

Our last night at the hospital together changed me. That aroma of sickness, human suffering, medicine, sterile utensils on trays, and hospital food was something I never wanted to sense again. I realized I would never feel comfortable in a hospital, and I soon acknowledged that all the money in the world couldn't make me want to work in one.

Uncertain about what to do next, I still attended classes while I tried to think things through. In American History II, a prerequisite for my degree, I listened as my teacher, Professor Lillian Harris, a former Peace Corps volunteer, started her lecture. But on that day she paused in her lesson plan to make a simple, yet profound, statement. She seemed to be looking straight at me when she said, "What matters more than money in a job is peace of mind." Her simple words touched my soul.

I drove home in a blue funk, tossing these words around my weary mind. By the time I reached the house, I knew what I had to do. To get that "peace of mind," I would have to return to the plan I'd had for myself when I was younger, when I hadn't had to think about money. When I was 18 years old, graduating from high school, I had wanted to be a history teacher. I wanted to be in a classroom with kids and be a part of the learning process. But instead of continuing on to college, I married young and became a wife and mother. Teaching history had been a shelved dream; I was about to dust it off and make it happen.

When I got home I was crying, almost delirious with relief because I finally knew what I wanted and why I wanted it. My husband assumed my tears were for my mother, and probably thought my ever-present grief had rattled my thinking when I told him I wanted to become a teacher. This was a job that my heart cried out for, I told him. He must have decided it was not a good time to question my decision-making faculties, because all he said was, "Okay."

I think there was a tad of a question in that "okay" but his eyes were kind; his look was sympathetic. What in the world was he really thinking? What in this world was I thinking?

I told him this would mean more years of school in a completely new major. Again he said, "Okay."

He had been a man of one word when I announced my decision through my tears, but his actions spoke volumes after I executed it. He became "Mr. Mom" and took over housecleaning, cooking and reading bedtime stories when I was closeted away, cramming for exams. His attitude was always positive, never letting me down. I would never have made it without him. He held me up while I was starting over.

Every day, for three more years, I drove back and forth from

Mississippi to the University of Memphis, but this time it was for a degree that I wanted for the right reasons.

Finally graduation day arrived, and before I knew it I was walking across the stage and accepting my diploma. I could hear my family cheering for me. By then I had six children, and they were all there, along with their father, incredibly proud of me. Beaming, glowing, I waved. I could even feel my mother's presence. I was 42.

Before my state certification came through, I got a job teaching first graders at a little Montessori school in Memphis. They were sweet children, greeting me every morning with little comments like, "Mrs. Marrs, you have on blue eye shadow. Mrs. Marrs, you look tired. Mrs. Marrs, we love you." On the last day of school, two of the girls, Natalie and Candace, held my hands and wiped their tears with the hem of my dress. These children really cared about me. Little did I know that this kind of experience would hardly be the norm.

Over the next eight years, I worked at three different schools as an English teacher at junior high or high school level. History teaching positions were hard to find, I'd learned, as schools facing budget cuts would double up, hiring their school coaches to pinch-hit as history teachers. So I was happy to find a job as an English teacher.

Still, just being a teacher at my first two tough schools jeopardized my safety. A colleague once called me over to her classroom across the hall. I watched her take out a small vial of oil and then slowly walk around, stopping at each desk to trace the sign of the cross on its top. I gave her an inquisitive look and she said, "You'll see."

And I did, when a student assaulted me during roll call.

I changed jobs once again, accepting a position to teach English at an alternative school, populated by "bad" kids transferred out of ordinary schools. The alternative school specialized in discipline and instruction techniques especially crafted for difficult students, and since I *knew* standard teaching wasn't working, I wanted to see if anything would.

The job turned out to be a blessing.

Time and time again I encountered students from sad backgrounds who had made some wrong choices, turning to crime or drugs, but now wanted to change for the better. The school's barrier-breaking philosophy reached out to many of these "problem children," but ultimately it was the kids themselves who saved me as a teacher because they *wanted* to learn.

Is it easy? Not by a long shot. But it's worthwhile. I love what I do! And my income, although modest—it's still Mississippi—is more meaningful than ever. My husband, who has been diagnosed with degenerative spinal arthritis, can only play music occasionally, leaving me as the main family support.

What I tell anyone who asks is: Follow your heart. Listen to that little voice inside you and go after your career dream. That, God willing, is the route to inner peace. Do not be afraid to make changes in your life. It's never too late. Never too late.

Judith Z. Marrs teaches English at the Desoto County Alternative Center in Hernando, Mississippi. She and her husband, Don Marrs, are the proud parents of six children, ages 13 to 35.

SECTION III

♦ SEARCHING FOR A SOULMATE ♦

Illman Brothers

"Love is not a union merely between two creatures; it is a union between two spirits."
— FREDERICK W. ROBERTSON

THROUGH SOME ILL-FITTING TIME AND SPACE

James Tipton

Through some ill-fitting time and space

he wandered, carrying in a pack

what tenderness and little bread he had

until the bread was gone, at last arriving

only to this: a love that had no skin,

no rocking bed, no breakfast by the sea.

But what if he on earth was born

to find the woman of his heart

and love her greatly? What matter

then that space disjointed conjured all

against him? What matter then

the loneliness of flesh?

What if the one fine purpose

of his poor and complicated life

had been to wander through

the masquerades of love, the mean

and lowly lies, deceits, and empty hearts,

and still survive?

Yes, survive, despite the brutal wives,

their lives of lies and callous laughter,

survive to seek what he had always sought,

so much that no career and nothing

of importance ever happened in his life,

but this:

He found the woman of his heart

and loved her greatly; loved her so

that in a thousand years some dusty scholar

might unearth some letters, gentle lines

of love as in the ancient lore, and pausing

for a moment think,

This was a man who found the woman

of his heart, and loved her greatly.

Reprinted from James Tipton's Letters from a Stranger, *winner of the 1999 Colorado Book Award.*

TWO RIGHTS ADD UP

Lori D. Ward

I first met Barry during the hottest part of a humid North Carolina summer six years ago, when he parked his truck in the Montgomery County Library parking lot, next to my car. It was about two-thirty in the afternoon, and I was reading while having a late lunch in my beaten up Taurus. With a sandwich in one hand and a book in the other, I looked up when I heard an engine next to my window, and was amazed to see a short version of Indiana Jones, brown fedora hat included, getting out of a beat-up yellow-beige pickup. I was immediately attracted to this man. Besides looking like Harrison Ford, he had a fabulous physique, as well as laugh lines crinkling at the corners of otherwise youthful eyes. They are a cool shade of pale blue—a color I've never seen on anyone else before or since. I wasn't looking for a man that sultry afternoon of my 24th summer, as I was embroiled in an on-again, off-again relationship with someone. But watching this wonderful specimen leave his truck, I wished that I were unattached.

I registered that he had been tanned dark by the sun. I also noted that he was coated in grime and dust, and sweating profusely as he shifted a variety of strange tools from the truck bed into a lock-box on the back of the pickup. When he came around to the passenger side of his truck he nodded and said hello. I didn't want it to end there, so I quickly asked him a question about his work. He gave me a brief rundown of his job as a "soil scientist" for the U.S. Agriculture Department. This basically meant he spent a lot of time tromping in the deep woods, digging up soil and determining its type. The weird tools included a hand auger that he used to bring up soil cores.

As he locked up, he told me that he was on his way to report his findings. The office to which he was headed was in a building next to the library where I worked.

I was 20 minutes late getting back to my job as a technical assistant, but meeting Barry was more than worth it. And I wanted to see him again. But I had a problem. I had taken an unusually late lunch that day, but my usual break was from noon to one, which meant that I wouldn't be able to talk to Barry again when he got back at around two the next day. That afternoon I rearranged my lunch time for the foreseeable future so that I would be outside when Barry came back from his fieldwork. (I later learned that Barry had also altered his hours so that he could be in by two!)

With our schedules aligned, we were able to meet every day to chat. I learned that Barry was 31, and gleaned a few other personal details. Most often, we talked about activities and hobbies. He was surprised to learn that I loved fishing and had my own rod, reel, and tackle box and, yes, that I baited my own hook. One day, he mentioned that bow season was coming up and that he would have to spend the weekend at target practice to get ready. When I asked him whether his bow was compound or recurve, his jaw dropped open at the realization that I knew the difference. Though I didn't hunt, I liked shooting at targets and had my own bow at home.

After Barry discovered my love of pottery, he mentioned he was planning to ride out to Seagrove, a nearby town that is nationally known for its hundreds of potters. Barry routinely gave pottery as gifts, and he wanted to do some early Christmas shopping. He invited me to join him, and offered to pick me up at my house. We spent a companionable day enjoying the fall scenery and visiting several shops. Talking over lunch at the Jugtown Café, we found common ground in religion and our thoughts on the importance of family. We didn't agree on everything, of course, but our viewpoints on major issues were similar.

Throughout the day I kept waiting for some signal from him about whether this was a friendly get-together or a date, but it didn't materialize. He never once tried to kiss me or even hold my hand. I didn't realize then how old-fashioned Barry was in his approach to courting. Later, I'd learn that he had felt that showing affection on a first date would have been inappropriate. But, at the time, I took his reserve as a sign he wanted to keep the relationship strictly platonic. Disappointed, I must have been a little less ebullient during our next lunchtime encounter, because, as I also learned later, after our outing he confided to his friends that I had "cooled" toward him, which he took as a sign that *I* wanted to be just friends. Talk about mixed reviews! We weren't on the same page when it came to romance.

Our slow-moving relationship was about to come to a standstill.

Barry, believing that family came first, no longer had much time to spare as his chronically ill father began to really deteriorate. Meanwhile, my own intermittent, troubled romance had me in an emotional turmoil, and I just couldn't seem to get that closure I needed to signal my interest in Barry.

Then, for work reasons, Barry moved to a town three hours away. We exchanged Christmas cards and letters every now and then. With each one, I hoped something more would develop between us but that wasn't slated to happen right then.

Once in a while Barry stopped in at the library on his way to visit his family. Those brief hellos delighted me because I knew they meant an hour's detour for Barry, but I hesitated to make too much of them. And, sure enough, the visits dwindled until they stopped altogether.

Barry and I lost contact. A few years passed. The hope for the romance with Barry that might have been, faded from my heart.

I was lonely and I prayed, asking God to send me the one He had chosen for me.

Then came the Christmas I was in charge of my church's annual children's program. One Wednesday night I worked late then rushed home to load my car with all the necessary props and copies of the freshly rewritten scripts. As I scrambled to get everything together, the doorbell rang, and I groaned. When I opened the door, my aggravation turned immediately to regret— regret that I had to leave.

Barry stood on my doorstep, his grin spreading all the way up to those pale blue eyes. "I wasn't even sure you'd still live here, but decided to give it a shot on my way to my Mom's. Thought you might like to go get some dinner."

All I could get out at first was: "I'm so glad to see you but I've really gotta go."

Then I collected myself and briefly explained the situation of the moment. And I invited him to come to the children's program with me. Barry, always easygoing, understood perfectly. He didn't come with me, but he asked for a rain check on dinner.

After Christmas, he called to ask me for lunch. That lunch date marked a definite transition from friendship to romance, and we both knew it. But it was not until our fifth date, when Barry and I kissed for the first time that I began to suspect that old Barry was the new man I'd been praying for.

Still, we took our new relationship slowly, seeing each other only once or twice a month because we still lived a good three hours' drive apart. But we also called each other regularly and e-mailed each other often.

Some things, however, needed to be said face to face. One night as we sat on my sofa, I asked Barry, "What made you come back after all that time?"

He replied, "God," without further explanation. I knew then Barry was *the* one.

I was certain that Barry was going to propose to me, but as

WORLDLY WISDOM

A heart that loves is always young.—Greek saying

Who travels for love finds a thousand miles is not longer than one.—Japanese proverb

Even in Paradise, it's not good to be alone.
—Jewish folk saying

Christmas approached without Barry uttering those magic words, I told myself that he was probably saving them for my birthday in July. The truth was I was too happy to worry about it.

I celebrated Christmas with Barry at his mother's house, where presents were piled high. And I guessed that my present would not be pottery when I saw, with my name on it in Barry's writing, the distinctively shaped box Barry's brother-in-law uses to package the steppingstones he handcrafts as a hobby. These stones are works of art, each inlaid with a stained glass design.

And, sure enough, when I opened the box it contained a beautiful rose steppingstone. But tucked next to it was a little jewelry box. I looked into the box and saw a princess-cut diamond ring. The ring was Barry's proposal, which I joyously accepted for all to hear.

Six months later, before even more witnesses, I said, "I do," without a quiver of doubt. The right time had come for me to marry the right man.

Lori D. Ward resides in Henderson, North Carolina, with her husband and their two dogs, Cassie and Rusty. She enjoys swimming, boating, fishing, but not jogging—but she does it anyway.

BALM OF TRUE LOVE
Criselda Yabes

I had a satisfying career as a journalist, globetrotting in search of the latest story, until I was unexpectedly crippled by heartache and despair. I had gone to Moscow with a man whom I thought was my soul mate, a fellow reporter with whom I'd been for seven years. We'd gone to report on the fall of Communism, but the important story to me turned out to be that he'd found someone else. He ended our relationship by leaving me cold and alone, smack in the middle of Red Square, while he went off with his new love, a Lithuanian guide.

I returned only briefly to my native city, Manila, where I accepted a scholarship to study in Paris. I hoped the new surroundings would help heal my devastated heart. Paris was a beautiful place to spend time but after the money from my scholarship ran out, I couldn't stay. Still depressed, I flew back to the Philippines. I moved into a new, small apartment in Manila, which sat on a hill overlooking a valley of suburban factories, and I tried to put my life back together.

But I couldn't. I found myself emotionally paralyzed, choosing to sit by the window, pretending to see the Parisian skyline, and imagining happier times. I rarely left my apartment except to visit my therapist or to take out the trash.

I had a limited number of visitors, one of whom was an Indian lover who promised he would leave his wife for me. I knew entangling myself with him was wrong but he was a caring man and I was grasping for anyone who could rebuild my confidence.

I cried every day. On Sundays I could hear the echoes of churchgoers in the valley singing, "God have mercy on me," and I would rock back and forth in my chair, singing along through my tears.

Money became a problem. I couldn't land a job in my condition but I tried. The series of professional rejections only made things worse. My bank account was dwindling; I was living on the equivalent of $100 a month, surviving on milk and peanut butter sandwiches.

In an attempt to both make a little money and purge my despair, I wrote a book, *A Journey of Scars,* about my experiences in Moscow and Paris. Its publication alienated friends and family. They said it was too raw, too honest. Their reactions made me unable to return to my keyboard. Writer's block added to my woes. If I couldn't write, what was there to live for? Another bad love? Another man?

My country has a tradition of acknowledging a man's indiscretions. These relationships are called *kabits* meaning "attachments." I wavered between believing that as a *kabit* I was the loved one, and trying to break free of my married lover. Each time I tried to leave him, he begged me to stay, showering me with flowers and poetry. Too weak-willed to make him stay away for good, I took him back.

My therapist put me on anti-depressants. I desperately wanted my path straightened, beautified like Manila's Dewey Boulevard with its neatly arranged palm trees. I kept looking for a "fix" for my state of mind, consulting numerous therapists besides my regular one. I also joined New Age workshops. I treated these ventures, these hours spent outside my apartment, as markers on my road to recovery. But there were no real signs that I was getting any better.

Finally, the big day arrived: My lover's marriage fell apart. When he telephoned me I should have been happy that we could finally—after two and a half years—be openly together. But what he really wanted was reassurance that I was still around for *him:* he offered me no commitment in return. An unexpected angel

The Sick Girl by Edvard Munch

must have been perched on my shoulder the day he called. I took a deep breath and instead of saying "I love you," I said, "Please stop calling me. I want you out of my life."

I hung up the phone, stunned. But I couldn't deny that the words had come straight from my soul.

From then on, my spirit took flight. I'd been able to shake off my dependence on the idea of love. My lover was now free to love whomever he wanted but I'd finally made the decision to do what was best for *me*.

My writing came back. I stopped taking anti-depressants. I flew to several islands and wrote two more books. I saved my money and rewarded myself with a trip to Paris.

I first saw my future husband in the neighborhood pool in Montmartre. He was tall and thin, with sharp Mediterranean features that attracted me. He stopped the happy song he was humming to invite me for a cup of hot chocolate.

We began to talk. I learned that he was a French pharmacist

who likes to mountain climb. He had been a wanderer like me; he had done humanitarian work as a pharmacist in Africa, and we were able to talk about travel and different cultures. He seemed mellow and relaxed, but I learned that he used to be a firebrand, full of challenge for anyone or anything, and that his current calm was the result of learning how to take each day as it came. Like me, he had been wounded by past relationships. Neither of us expected to find love again.

For perfect strangers, we were remarkably similar; two people worn out by turmoil, both returning to our favorite city, Paris.

Almost two months later, he followed me to the Philippines. Our Parisian romance gave way to reality, which is what a real love story is about, a story about building a solid foundation for a lasting relationship.

We've been married for three years.

My husband is the opposite of the men of my past. When we are together I am so certain that I am loved. It's as simple as that.

We live in Paris and are hoping to start a family. Whenever we feel burdened by the world around us, or either of us somehow feels inadequate, we take long walks on the banks of the Seine or ride around the city on his scooter, stopping to sit in a park or café to talk.

After we've solved a problem or resolved a difference, we tell each other, "Thank you." Thank you for being here with me.

Criselda Yabes, who has worked for the AP and Reuters, is the author of four books.

COURTING KELLY
Marty Burke

Hey, Kelly, when are you going to go out with me?" I asked in my most winning voice. "Never," she said without a pause.

"I think you're afraid that you might find you like me. I promise you, just one date, and you'll never want anyone else."

"Not interested," she said, with the emphasis on "not."

Courting Kelly was an uphill battle. I had begun to woo her soon after graduating from high school. She was only older than I was by about 17 months, but she had made it clear that she considered me incredibly immature. Each time she shot me down I would put on a show of bravado to hide my hurt, and declare, "I guess I'm just too much man for you, but you'll grow up someday." I refused to give up because I knew that when I looked at Kelly I saw everything that I wanted in a lifelong friend and partner. She had confidence, strength, beauty and a smile that would break like day on a clear morning. But I just kept doing or saying the wrong things.

We both worked at the Winn Dixie on Aloma Avenue in Winter Park, Florida, so I saw her every day. One day I popped by her workstation and caught her by surprise. "You look like an elf," I said. This was meant as a compliment. At the time I was into the genre of fantasy and had a deep respect for elves.

"Like a what?" she asked with an edge to her voice.

"Well, just then, you were looking down and your hair was hanging over your ears, and I got the impression of an elf in my mind, and thought it fit you." She looked at me as though I were an alien with three heads. I thought that she must have confused elves with trolls, or something like that, because who could be offended by being called an elf?

"You think I look like an elf?" she queried. "Are you crazy? Is this your way of trying to win me over? If it is, you're crazy!"

"Does this mean that you still don't want to go out on a date with me?" I asked, genuinely feeling misunderstood. I spent the rest of my breaks that day trying to persuade her that comparing her to an elf was meant to flatter her. She just refused to see it.

Not only did I say the wrong things but I was definitely not her type. I had a bit of a wild attitude, a mustache that was not in fashion, and a radio in my car that let you know minutes ahead of time that I was on my way. I would make the glass rattle when I pulled into the parking lot just to let her know I was at work. "Did you hear me?" I would ask.

She would say, "No!"

The manager informed me: "If you keep that up, I'll cut your hours!"

I also wore my hair long, which she said she hated.

But I wouldn't give up. I was convinced that I could still show Kelly that I was someone that she should get to know.

That year, Kelly enrolled in the University of Central Florida while she worked part time. She had less time for me than before and would turn me down flat with "I am in college and have absolutely no time for a boyfriend or dating. There is no way I will ever go out with you."

I called this the "No-Hope-Treat-Him-Cold Phase."

I met her between classes one day, and said, "You know, you really are wearing me down. I need something to go on here; otherwise I might have to stop asking you out. Is there any hope? I mean, even a little tiny bit of hope?" She thought for a moment and said, "A friend once told me that persistence wears out resistance."

I decided to stay persistent.

It was the summer of 1994 when we finally reached a compromise. We all had the same friends, and the summertime meant trips to the beach. I put my friends up to lobbying her on my behalf to come with me to the beach. Kelly couldn't say that she didn't have time since classes weren't in session, and Florida's heat made one long for the ocean. We reached an agreement that Kelly would come with her friend Sharon, while I would bring along a guy friend. We had a good time and our beach foursome got to be a regular thing.

Every weekend, the four of us would jump in my Pontiac Grand Prix and grab lunch at the beach. We had some great times. One time the song "Cold as Ice" just happened to be playing and I made a comment like "Hey, Kel, it's your theme song."

We all laughed; then she put me in my place by telling me not to call her "Kel."

Then the Rolling Stones' song, "I'm so hot for her she's so cold," came on and I had to pull over until the laughing subsided.

Over the months, Kelly and I grew closer. Every time we went to the beach I would ask her if she wanted to walk with me down to the pier; finally one day she said yes. We walked amidst hundreds of people, but I felt as if we were the only two people on the planet. When we got to the pier I asked her if she would go on a date with me, just the two of us.

She answered, "Well, I guess we could go out once, but only once. I don't want you to get your hopes up that there will be a second date."

I reached down and tried to hold her hand. She fought it for a minute and then let me. We were far enough away that our friends wouldn't see.

For a few minutes, we walked in silence. She was probably wondering if she was doing the right thing. I was on cloud nine.

Our romance started that day but we hid it from our co-workers for months.

About three months after our important walk, I bought her a promise ring. The ring was tri-color gold—pink, white, and yellow—with three intertwining hearts, for past, present and future. Even though it only cost a little over a hundred dollars, that was a big amount for me back then, and I hoped that when she saw it she would understand that I was growing up into a man who could commit to a real relationship.

On the night I planned to give her the ring and declare my love, I took her to a romantic seaside restaurant. We had a nice dinner and then went down to the beach for another walk. I gave her the ring and told her not just "I love you," but that she made my soul complete. We confessed our love to each other, and I knew our feelings to be true the minute she voluntarily placed her hand in mine.

Marriage didn't happen right away. It took me three more years to finally take myself off to college, lagging behind Kelly, who had finished before I'd even started. In my junior year of college I proposed, and once I graduated a year later, we married. The happy date was July 19th, 1997. Three years later, our son, Dylan, was born, and he is a constant joy. I got a job teaching English at a nearby high school, and when I look at myself now, with a steady job and a family, I see a responsible adult and not the unruly misfit I once was. My wife now lets me call her Kel, but to this day she's never understood the elf compliment thing.

Marty Burke and his family make their home in Orlando, Florida.

SEDUCTION BY POETRY
Sherry L. Stoll

I met Daryl on a blind date on February 1, 1997. I liked him from the moment I saw him. He met me at the door with the most beautiful smile I had ever seen. He was a country gentleman—tall, dark and handsome. I wondered what on earth he would see in me. He seemed to have all the right moves as he opened doors and chatted easily. I was nervous and insecure, especially about my appearance. I'm what one would call a "full-figured woman," and I was losing hope that I would find someone who didn't dismiss me because of my weight.

Daryl and I had been set up by mutual friends. If he was as nervous as I was, he never showed it.

Through the course of the evening, I discovered Daryl farmed and raised cattle in addition to packaging batteries at Energizer. He was a cowboy deep down. Despite my nervousness, he made me feel at ease. I had a good time and believed Daryl and I had clicked. I thought that I'd hear from him soon.

But I didn't.

I lived in Rock Port, Missouri, about 45 miles from Daryl's home. I waited and waited for him to call. I don't know why I didn't give up. I considered calling him but, between his job and his cattle, I thought I probably wouldn't reach him and wouldn't know quite what to say if I did. So, I sent him a thank-you note, and included a poem I had written called "The Wallflower and The Rose," which described how, after the beautiful scent of the rose fades away, the wallflower remains steady and strong.

A month went by and I still had heard nothing from him. I wondered how my impression of our time together had been so awry. Obviously, I thought, Daryl had found something wrong with me. It had to be my weight.

I sent another letter with another poem. It wasn't like me to do this. A greater power had to be pushing me.

This time, Daryl responded. He called me and asked me to a cowboy poetry gathering. I accepted, but then my insecurity kicked in. I was sure it was a mercy date. Here I had been pursuing this poor man through the U.S. mail. Surely this date was to get me off his back.

We had a lot of fun at the cowboy poetry gathering. Daryl actually liked poetry. My heart fluttered. I got to see Daryl's sensitive side when a tear trickled down his cheek during the recital of a poem about an old rancher who'd lost his farm to the bank.

After another couple of weeks of silence, I sent Daryl another letter and poem. I kept it light and told him this would be my last letter. I would leave him alone. The rest was up to him. I told him that I knew I wasn't the most beautiful woman on the face of the earth, but I was sincere, with a good heart.

Another week passed. I spent a beautiful Easter Sunday with my family then returned to my empty apartment. Thinking of

Daryl, I murmured a very simple prayer. "Lord, I really like him. If we are meant to be together, could I at least hear from him today?" Five minutes later, the phone rang. It was Daryl, asking if I was busy the following weekend.

We made plans and then talked for a while. Daryl said he really liked my letters and poems. I couldn't believe how quickly my prayer had been answered.

"Thank you, Lord," I said after I hung up the phone.

From then on, we dated steadily on weekends. Without fail, during our courtship, I sent him a letter and a poem each week. Many of them were poems about cowboys.

As our relationship developed, I knew I had to find out the truth about what Daryl thought about my weight. I asked him if that was the reason he hadn't contacted me for so long after our initial meeting. He told me that he would be lying if he said no. But he added that I had impressed him on that date, and that my follow-up letters and poems revealed to him what a sweet lady he was missing out on. He said he thought he'd better get in gear before someone else snatched me up.

His honesty touched me. We were in love.

When Daryl proposed to me a few months after our blind date, I accepted, confident that he loved me for exactly who I am.

We recently celebrated our fourth wedding anniversary, and my husband remains my true love—and muse. We moved to his grandparents' homestead after our marriage, and now have purchased it. We still go to the cowboy poetry gathering, too. Verse brought us together and will always be a part of our life.

Sherry L. Stoll, former managing editor of Herbal/Organic.com, is now a busy ranch wife.

LOVE AT FIRST BYTE

Amber McMillan

Love was for dreamers, not for a single mother with a six-month-old daughter. My brain told me: Forget about meeting anyone, let alone someone special; I would remain housebound until my daughter became old enough for day care. As much as I might hope for companionship, that seemed impossible, unless that someone special mysteriously materialized in my living room.

During my marriage, my brother-in-law had shown me how to log on to the Internet. After the divorce, I had to find a way to support the two of us without benefit of alimony or child support checks. My main source of income came from proofreading manuscripts in my home, but I occasionally wrote monologues for a drama teacher in California, or entered poetry contests with cash prizes.

One big expense turned out to be clothing for my ever-growing girl. Prowling Yahoo Auctions one day, I realized that many people sold their children's clothes. I decided to try it. As soon as my daughter outgrew something, I'd post it, sell it, and use the money to buy her clothes in a bigger size. To my surprise, more often than not, I would make a profit. That small income, along with the freelance writing jobs, allowed me to pay our bills.

Splitting my days between caring for my daughter and using my computer, I fell into surfing the net in my free time, using the name "bumber1," a spin-off of a nickname from my childhood. I soon met other single mothers online, and we become each other's virtual shoulders to lean on. One night, after getting my daughter off to bed, I logged on as usual and entered a chat room. As I was typing away, someone Instant Messaged me. Instant Messages can become very annoying because they pop up on your screen no matter what you are doing. You can close the window, but if you are Instant Messaged again, it just pops up again and again unless you block that person. Anyway, three hours into my chat session, I received an Instant Message from someone with the screen name of R22637A. I didn't know that tag and became more wary when I learned my instant caller was a man. Many users trawl the net looking for sex and whatnot, and I was definitely not interested.

I typed him a curt message and closed the window. But he immediately replied, "I don't want to talk about sex. We can talk about anything; I am actually a real person. What is your name?"

This time, I didn't immediately blow him off, and we began to chat. We ended up sharing our life stories. We stayed online until 3AM.

I marveled at how different we were. He'd had a relatively stable home life, with a psychologist and a teacher for parents, who'd stayed married into his teens. I didn't know my father, and my mother's boyfriend and I didn't get along at all. R22637A had gone to college; I had received my GED at 15 and married young. Only recently had college begun to interest me. I had been in and out of relationships; my chat-line friend said he'd had a few long-term girlfriends. His biggest regrets ranged from wishing that he had gone to graduate school to wishing that he'd been closer to his father. Mine were more along the lines of wishing that I hadn't tried that drug or testified against that person. We were like night and day.

Days passed and we continued to chat. Soon, he was asking if we could talk on the phone. I always said no, insisting that I wasn't going to give my number to someone I'd met on the Internet. I was afraid because it seemed to me that I was already half in love with this man. I'd told my sister about this burgeoning romance, and she warned me to be careful. I think a part of me never wanted to talk to him on the phone for fear it would burst the image I had of him. I worried that I had created an image of him that was not true to life.

But he wouldn't wait forever. With a 900-mile gap between us, and no possibility of us running into each other at the grocery store and setting up a date, he was growing impatient.

One evening, almost a full year after the first night we chatted, I came online to see him there, waiting. Immediately, he asked if he could call me. At that point I had come close to letting him call me a few times, so we had exchanged phone numbers. I turned him down, expecting us to go on chatting.

Instead he messaged me, "Well I am home if you want to talk. Bye." All of a sudden, I saw his name go from bold to normal text, indicating that he was now offline. My stomach dropped to the floor. I flew to the phone, dialing the numbers so quickly that it seemed as though I had dialed them a thousand times before. The phone was suddenly ringing very loudly in my ear. Then he picked up.

"Hello," a surprisingly beautiful male voice said at the other end.

'Hello," I said.

"Who is this," he asked.

"Who do you think this is?"

"You called me."

"It's me."

"Well hello there . . . finally." And we began to talk.

We met face to face almost a month to the day of our first phone call.

He flew to my city. Since he didn't know the area, we'd agreed that I would pick him up at his hotel and then go out for lunch. As I drove over a bridge that separated us I thought to myself, *I must be crazy.* I was in love with a man whom I had never seen face-to-face. As I neared the hotel, I thought about turning around. After I finally made myself park, I got out of the car and looked up at the massive building, which seemed to be looming over me like a father telling me to go home. But, I figured, I had come this far; I couldn't turn back now. Besides, I really did want to meet him, hold his hand, see his eyes while we talked.

As I went up the stairs my heart was thumping so loudly in my chest I thought I was going to have a heart attack. I took a deep breath before I knocked at his door. Less than a full second later, he answered.

My breath was definitely gone then.

He was gorgeous. His skin was a soft cocoa color. His eyes were deep brown, like mahogany. He had light brown curls that softly sat on his head. He was very clean-cut, freshly shaven, and he smelled good.

He smiled and hugged me. I know he could feel my heart beating wildly in my chest because I could feel his beneath his freshly starched shirt. When we were finally able to sit down and talk, it only took a few minutes before I felt as if we'd known each other for years. I later learned that he had felt the same way at that first meeting.

As time went on, he visited more and more and I allowed him to meet my daughter. The three of us were very comfortable together and, after a year of his visits, she started calling him Daddy.

It was then that he officially proposed. It seemed like the natural progression of our relationship, since I already felt that we were bonded for life. We were married a year and a half after we met; I became pregnant shortly after that. We lost that baby but started trying for the next, and in late 2000 we learned that, if all went well, we'd have a child in August of 2001. Our son was born on the ninth of the predicted month, and he is the spitting image of my husband.

"*To love for the sake of being loved is human, but to love for the sake of loving is angelic.*"
—Alphonse de Lamartine

Paul Klee

I find myself unexpectedly blessed with a loving and caring family. My little girl smiles when she talks about how far we've come together. My husband supports me in every way, as he has done from day one, and our son is a ray of sunshine. I could say I am now a firm believer in love at first byte. It worked for me.

Amber McMillan and her family make their home in St. Petersburg, Florida.

SECTION IV

◆ Finding a Real Home ◆

The Old Stone House, Currier

*"The home to everyone is to him his castle
and fortress, as well for his defense against
injury and violence, as for his repose."*
— Edward Coke

FOUR WALLS AND A FAMILY
Tara Waller

I was an American-born Korean child in search of a home. My birth mother had given me up for adoption some months after my first birthday, which resulted in my falling into the hands of the Children's Services Division in Oregon. I was shuffled from one "placement" to another as it became evident, time and again, that I had not yet found a healthy home.

When I was eight, my sixth family found me: a mom, dad, and 13-year-old brother. I was told that I was to live with them for a year; at the end of that time, I could make my own decision about staying. The trailer that my new family had been living in before I arrived was too small, and the family—*my family?*—began to construct a house to include me. In early spring, we moved into the first floor of our two-story house, one that my new father was building with his own hands. By hanging sheets of the heavy black plastic, Visqueen, he'd made makeshift rooms while we waited for the solid walls to go up.

My new dad, a well-built firefighter, frightened me. Fathers in my past had been abusive; some had wanted more from me than just being a daughter, and I didn't know if he would be any different. I also wondered about my new mother, whose quiet nature was foreign to me after the physical and emotional abuse past "mothers" had inflicted upon me. Watching over me every day, my new mother fed and clothed me, and I soon learned that every time she did something special it was her way of saying "I love you." My brother was a mystery to me. I liked him, but his threats of letting his pet garter snake loose in my bed made me keep a wary eye on him.

I knew as much about being a kid in a loving family as I knew about how to build a house. I didn't know what "normal" child-parent behavior was, and I was scared. I didn't know what was expected of me. Like the heavy plastic that walled in my bedroom, much of my life had been dark and unstable. I'd learned that if I didn't trust what was going on, or if someone made me unsure, I had to try to stand up for myself.

One day my dad unexpectedly asked me to make lunch.

"I don't know how to cook," I replied matter-of-factly.

"You can learn. A tuna sandwich is easy. Try it," he said.

"I don't know how to make a tuna sandwich and I don't want to," I retorted.

This did not go over well with my dad. He was so mad he threatened to spank me. My first thought was that he was going to be like the others, and that all the abuse would start up again. But he surprised me. He calmed down, then patiently explained "the art" of a good tuna sandwich. This clear explanation was about more than about a simple sandwich; it was about trust. I gained a new understanding of what it meant to be a part of a giving family.

On February 25, 1985, I officially became a part of this family. Throwing me a party to celebrate my adoption, they showered me with loving attention as well as many wonderful gifts. Among these was a teddy bear. He was someone to cuddle, to listen to my problems, to soak up my tears and to be a faithful friend. Whenever I stumbled, as I continued to learn how to be part of a family, my little bear was there to comfort me.

The house we were building was in the country. I hadn't cared where it was located; all I'd wanted was a place where I could stay put and be loved.

My father was a blueberry farmer in addition to being a fireman. Taking care of the bushes wasn't my idea of a good time, but they were there and I realized that I was going to have to learn to deal with them. As I found out more about growing blueberries, I also watched my house transform. Walls went up to replace the heavy plastic that had marked bedrooms, the living room, the kitchen, bathrooms and closets. Each completed step in the overall building process amazed me. The solid new walls that were erected seemed to mark the solidity of my position in my home and family. Both the blueberries and I thrived; I began to feel truly at home. The Oregon woods surrounded our property like old friends, outweighing the inconveniences of rural life; I was unashamed of where I lived and eager to defend it if necessary.

My high school was made up mostly of kids from the city, and they didn't understand why I liked living out in the country: "You live *there*?"

"Yes, there."

I'd just finished telling my school friends about our house. Most of them had only heard rumors about the area where I was from. "There" wasn't only the house, it was a town of a few hundred people where community was everything. Everyone knew each other. Everyone was friendly. There may have been acres of land around us, but the people formed a close-knit community. My classmates seemed to think that living in a small town meant that my family and I were somehow primitive, as if we couldn't possibly have electricity or indoor plumbing. No matter what they said, I loved living in the country, where everyone put a lot of stock in family, which for me wasn't something you gave up for the so-called benefits of city life.

My childhood years on our blueberry farm were happy ones for the most part. My parents were pleased that I was a good student and wanted me to go to college. My dad would have preferred that I attended the nearby community college but my mother wanted me to go to the best school I could, and was willing to work extra hours outside our home, to help pay for the private college in Salem I favored. My father came round to sup-

> *"Where we love is home, home that our feet may*
> *leave but not our hearts."*
> —Oliver Wendell Holmes

porting that decision. And so I went away to college.

I returned on my first winter break, eager to be coming home. To my surprise, our blueberry bushes were no longer there! My father had ripped them out because there was no one to help tend to them anymore. Oddly, I missed those blueberry bushes— the onetime bane of my existence. But I also recognized the symbolism of their removal. Just as the berries had grown up and been moved to another farm, so had I matured and gone on to another step in my life.

Now my parents are moving to another house that is smaller and more manageable for the two of them. We have all come to realize that our family has moved on. I will never again live in the house in which I grew up, but a home, when all is said and done, has little to do with where your property is or what grows on it. Even the sturdiest house means less than the bonds of love on which a true home rests.

Tara Waller and her husband live in Kyoto, Japan, where she is a web designer. She visits her family in Oregon at least once a year during the winter holidays.

WHERE THE HEART IS

Rosemerry Wahtola Trommer

Another lover might build you a castle—

a temple of stone with long mirror-lined halls

and a cadre of candles adorning the walls

to light your way through windowless nights.

Maybe there'd be a sinewy moat

to protect you from the wicked world,

and perhaps a tall tower for watching seasons pass.

Another lover might build you a mansion

filled with expensive vases and oversized chairs.

The high-ceilinged rooms would echo your voice,

and your lover would smile to hear you sing.

Tall doorways would frame you so strikingly,

and from each window long gardens would beckon you

to stroll amidst manicured rows.

But lover, I would build you a house in my heart

with a single story and an untamed yard. I'd make

a stone skirt using river rocks, each one smoothed by time.

The floors would be cherry, enduring, alive with

the memory of sunshine and bloom. Every window would

open to let in the wind, every door would swing wide

to deliver you in. And in the center room, a place for fire.

My husband, I'd build you a home in my heart

on a fast-moving river with fortified banks.

And there I would raise high the roof beams of gladness,

and there, I would lower the ceiling of sighs.

And there, in the warmth of my heart's kitchen

I would feed you and knead you and bake bread for you.

In the halls of my heart, I would welcome you home.

*Colorado inspirational speaker Rosemerry Wahtola Trommer is
the editor of the Virtue Victorious volume,* Charity: True Stories
of Giving and Receiving *and the author of two volumes of poetry.
You may visit more of her work at www.word-woman.com.*

HOPE LIVED HERE
Ina Proeber

I sat on the stoop and shucked the first ripe corn of the season. A car drove up the weedy driveway to our farm and stopped halfway, just beside the barn. A climbing honeysuckle my husband and I had planted beneath the stairs to the loft obscured part of my view. I could not read the license plate but sensed that those people came from far away. Their car looked too clean; no stubborn local red loam crusted its sides. Only a hint of salmon dust veiled the blue lacquer.

The sun was still high in the sky and glinted on the waters of the North Atlantic that edge my property. This was the time of day when the sea breeze shifted to a land breeze, and the water looked calmer. Shaded by my house behind me, I watched the sun's rays bounce off the tinted car windows and listened to the idling engine compete with the song of cicadas.

The engine shifted and the car moved forward. I decided not to stir. Curiosity about those strangers tied me to my spot.

I put down the cob I clutched in my hand and stood up. The passenger door swung open like magic, and a lady in shorts peeled herself off the seat. Her knees were as wrinkled as her face; on her bare arms, age spots reminded me of the splatters of boiled-over pumpkin soup. She smiled and let her gaze glide over to the barns. Her chest heaved as she took in a deep breath. I stood on the steps in awkward silence.

The elderly woman looked directly at me and introduced herself: "Hello, I'm Hope." I wondered if she and the driver had either lost their way or were canvassing religious ideas.

"I was born here on this farm, 77 years ago," Hope continued, "and wanted to see what had become of God's Little Acre. I'm Arthur Davey's sister."

My mind went back to shortly after we had moved into our rel-atively new farmhouse, not far from the sea, on Prince Edward Island. The outbuildings were much older, so it was in them I had looked for clues to the property's history. Had the farmers who'd lived here been happy? I'd hoped the nooks and crannies would yield clues.

I had climbed the old wooden stairs to the loft in the barn. Tall weeds hid its bottom steps and the posts were covered with lichen. It seemed important to know what had happened here to fully claim our new property as a home. The sheds were full of treasures: hand carved door latches; a plethora of fishing hooks; empty liquor bottles cunningly hidden between ceiling boards; and cryptic inscriptions on the walls. In the barn loft, I had read *A.L. Davey 1933*, written in oxblood on the board above a work-bench. Who was A.L. Davey? I didn't know.

"You are Arthur Davey's sister?" I repeated, easing myself back to the present, still wrestling with the surprise.

"Yes, I grew up here with him," Hope said, and I heard a quiver in her voice. "Did you buy the farm right after his death?"

"We came here only five years ago, but I have heard of Arthur. Arthur Davey. I found his name written on a barn wall. And other notes, too." I was excited. The history of our farm had arrived at our doorstep. "Some notes were about the old well," I remembered aloud. " 'Seventy feet deep, forty-five feet to the water.' Those were dated 1931."

Hope and her companion, Bob, strolled with me through the old barns, which were no longer in use but still smelled of live-stock. She told me about the black mare that used to stand in the big pen to the right and that only she was allowed to ride. Hope had to pause between sentences to swallow her emotions as childhood memories welled up.

I learned that a large cattle barn used to stand on the exact

WHAT PLACE WAS THIS?

Archeologists, exploring the ruins of a long-disappeared village or city, must ask: What was the purpose of a building unearthed?

In Junin, Peru, an archeological site 14,000 feet above sea level, John Rick, Associate Professor of Anthropological Sciences at Stanford University, decided that a mountain cave he was exploring had been a "habitation." Although it offered only about nine square feet of shelter, Dr. Rick was confident that he was looking at what once had been a dwelling because it contained a hearth—a place where fire had burned for warmth and cooking. Whether the cave had been a long-term home, or one used intermittently, perhaps by several generations of residents, is unknown.

Describing the use of a space is not always easy for Dr. Rick, who specializes in Andean culture. At Chavin de Huantar, also in Peru, 11,000 feet above sea level, he and fellow diggers had to carefully burrow six feet below the ground surface to open up a viewing area. Shards of pottery were plentiful, but that didn't necessarily mean that the archeologists were glimpsing an ancient dining room. Perhaps they were viewing part of a community storage area, a pottery workshop or something else. Since ancient Peruvians often used perishable substances, such as wattle and daub (canework and dirt), as building materials, the function of a space can be very difficult or impossible to determine.

While ancient sites around the world vary tremendously, some societies constructed houses in ways more helpful to contemporary researchers. Jennifer Perry, Professor of Archeology at Pomona College, cites the five-to-10,000-year-old buildings in Japan, which archeologists have identified as homes because of the stone-lined hearths built into their centers. According to Dr. Perry, the centrality of the fireplace underscores that such a home—large enough for an extended family—was likely more than just a shelter and feeding station. A central fireplace indicates a place where kin could also socialize and share important rituals.

Signs of occupancy need not be "writ" in stone in order to endure. Dr. Perry participated in a dig on San Clemente Island, the southernmost of the eight California Channel Islands west of San Diego, while she was investigating the nomads who frequented the area some 7,000 years ago. After digging through 5,000 feet of "rich, organic soil," Dr. Perry found "a layer of compacted soil made solid, like concrete, by trampling feet." Dr. Perry marvels that the layer of dirt was so strong that, "if you had taken a hammer to it, it wouldn't even necessarily break."

Further investigation indicated that a series of small structures, each no more than ten feet in diameter, had stood on these hard floors. The team of archeologists determined the outlines of these buildings from pieces of whalebone found near identifiable postholes. The whalebones would have been the frames for roofs and walls made of sea-mammal hides. Still, it was the discovery of hearths in the center of the hard earthen floors that signaled that these buildings had been residences.

Artifacts found at the site suggested that inhabitants had slept on mats woven from sea grass and kelp. Examination of the contents of an ancient trash pit near the residential area offered further evidence that people had dined within.

A simple hearth may only tell us that people once dwelled in a particular ruin or cave or building. A more complicated fireplace can reveal more about the daily lives of the people who warmed themselves before it. Mary C. Beaudry, Associate Professor of Archeology and Anthropology at Boston University, points out that the hearths of many colonial homes in Massachusetts and Virginia, as well as those found in houses of the same period or earlier in Scotland, are tall "enough for a person to stand up in," as well as several feet wide.

Why would the usually not very big central room of a single-family house need a large fire? The first answer is that the chimney of that era was not always efficient: Much of the heat escaped up it. (That's one reason why, a bit later on, affluent

(Continued on next page)

families embraced the newly invented Franklin stove.)

Dr. Beaudry reminds us that the large fireplace served not only to ward off seasonal chills and freezes but for cooking all year round. Cooks didn't prepare everything on one big blaze. Large fireplaces and ovens built into them supported "several small fires at once," says Dr. Beaudry. "You could have a bake fire, something going in the embers, and be cooking meat all at the same time."

The colonial homemaker was a multi-tasker, even as she prepared meals for as many as 20 people—her large family as well as additional farm laborers.

Tropical homes may lack interior hearths (or any newer heating system) if outdoor cooking is the custom. Still, more than any other single feature it is the hearth that marks a home.

The fireplace was the place where you warmed your feet or dried your clothes and where the calories needed to sustain human life were turned into meals. Warmth, in most places, is the essential quality of a home.

site of our Cape Cod style house, and that Hope's father had kept silver-fox cages where we'd built a deck, facing the sea. The three of us soaked in the spectacular view, and I mentioned the big rock guarding the cliff. Hope's eyes sparkled at that. Though she walked with arthritis stinging her knees, she said she'd like to see the big rock where she and Arthur had netted smelt and jigged mackerel. Not wanting to be intrusive, I let Bob help Hope down to the rock.

On my visitors' return, I welcomed them with tea and cookies on the retired lobster-trap-turned-coffee-table on the deck. As the sun descended over the patch of forest to the west and played with the hues of golden grain and red clover in the fields in front of us, I was still engrossed in Hope's tales of the old days when she had lived here. After Hope married, she and her husband had moved off the island, and her brother had taken over the farm. The land was the pride of Arthur's life, and Hope had kept close contact with her childhood homestead. Through letters, she'd taken part in every change, defeat and success Arthur had encountered.

As Hope talked, I was able to touch up with color the few gray images of the past that I had discovered in the undisturbed corners of the farm.

"I have an old photograph of the place in the '50s. I should send it to you," Hope said, as we walked back to the car.

After Hope and her friend had gone, I wondered if I'd expressed myself strongly enough so that she'd realize I wasn't just being polite when I said I'd love to have that picture. Could Hope see that we'd been planning for a long future here ever since we'd moved in, or had she been too engrossed with her own childhood memories to notice?

My husband and I had planted a new orchard after the tree-bending storms of our first autumn on the farm, and had continued to nourish the land in many other ways.

In the weeks following Hope's visit, my work about the farm assumed new meaning, invigorated by its links with the dreams of its long-ago owners. The information might not have meant as much to my husband, who had not met Hope, but you can't always tell what exactly fertilizes hard work.

However, the photo she'd promised didn't arrive and I half-forgot about it, too, as the sunny days and warm, star-littered nights gave way to chill autumn.

When the fields were brown and our trees bare, I finally found time to sit down to tidy my desk as a prelude to writing cards to distant friends. Buried under newspaper clippings, letters with foreign stamps, and gems from the beach, I found Hope's address on a ragged slip of paper, passed to me through the open car window on her departure.

I wrote to her, expressing thanks for her visit, now etched in my memory as the most memorable moment of the past summer.

The day before my 40th birthday, a letter arrived, addressed in old-fashioned, unfamiliar handwriting. When I opened the envelope, a watercolor card greeted me in the warm hues of summer. I recognized the two old apple trees in the front, the red barns in their practical symmetry, and the shimmering sea in the background. Enclosed in the beautifully colored card was nearly the same scene in a photograph, in black and yellowing white. Looking again at the watercolor, I saw that the painter had taken artistic license and altered the bordering white fences and revived an old vegetable garden. She had inscribed the mailbox, "HOPE."

The painting blurred in front of my misting eyes. The past merged with the present in my mind, enriching my surroundings.

Inside the card Hope had written, "Hope you have many happy years in your dream home in God's Little Acre. Love, Hope."

God's Little Acre—I hadn't really registered that this had been the Davey family's name for the farmstead that was now my home. It is still an apt name, and will live on through my husband and me.

Ina Proeber and her husband share "God's Little Acre," on Prince Edward Island, Canada, with two dachshunds, seven pet rabbits and approximately 40 goldfish in a man-made pond.

THIS NEW-OLD HOUSE
Hugh Howard

Everyone brings baggage—literal and otherwise—to the process of making a home. But my wife, Betsy, and I brought more than most. Our accumulated goods included a staircase, dozens of nineteenth-century doors and windows, a keg of antique nails and lots of old notions we wanted to recycle.

Our goal was to build a new-old house . . . and we succeeded, after a fashion. We've got the sound structure and up-to-date working systems of a new home, but the place looks as if it were built two centuries ago, with the shape and details of an early American house. It's got wavy glass in its windows and the door panels have the rippled contours of hand-planing.

This is a house packed with stories. Consider the staircase. We bought it from a Methodist parsonage that was about to be demolished. The place had been built just after the Civil War, a happy time for home construction because carpenters still knew how to do things by hand but factories were producing high-quality (affordable) machine-made goods. On first viewing, we knew the staircase was perfect: The newel post, balusters and railing were walnut, the finish original. The artifact bore the patina of age—the dents, scars, and wear marks of a well-used piece of antique furniture.

We weren't looking for new. We wanted some of the warmth and character of a true old house. Staircases once conveyed a great deal about a house and its status—or at least how seriously its builder wanted it to be taken. Our staircase was near the middle of that plain-to-fancy spectrum, a modest but serious statement by a capable nineteenth-century craftsman.

Our fireplace, in contrast, wouldn't be old, but a construct of bricks fresh from the brickyard. Yet its story reaches back

almost two hundred years to a New Hampshire soldier named Benjamin Thompson. Like his contemporary, Ben Franklin, he developed theories of thermodynamics decades before the term was even coined. His most memorable brainchild was the Rumford fireplace (the expatriate Thompson, in honor of his service to the elector of Bavaria, had become Count Rumford).

Today, Thompson's design is acknowledged as the most efficient and cleanest-burning fireplace. Its opening is tall, the firebox shallow, the chimney throat narrow. We got lucky, too, because the mason we hired brought with him a family history of masonry. From the weeds in his father's backyard he dug out a marble hearthstone that had once been a wainscot panel in a train station demolished in the 1960s. A good old idea, some vintage parts, and a gifted tradesman produced a focus for our living room.

We bought a pickup truck full of six-panel doors and six-over-six window sashes from a Connecticut dealer who was getting out of the business of selling architectural antiques and moving into cowboy memorabilia. The nails came from the janitor at my elementary school, who had gotten them from a hardware store where they had sat for about a hundred years. To him, they were outmoded and useless. But those flattened cut nails were just what would have been used to build a dwelling like ours in the nineteenth century.

For the frontispiece of our house we found an elegant, Federal-style doorway. Even seeing it in pieces, sitting on the first floor of a rotting carriage shed, we knew we had to have it. The door was an imposing seven feet tall. Constructed in an age when American craftsmen were reviving classical architectural elements, the elaborate frame featured flattened columns, a tall cornice, hand-shaped moldings, and delicate rosettes that, we guessed, had once been gilded.

At auctions and from other dealers we came up with a couple of marble sink surrounds, several antique light fixtures, and lots of latches and locks. But putting all these historical parts to use involved more than assembly. We had to configure a unique design to integrate the disparate elements—the stairs and doorway had to bookend one another in the main hall, for example. We didn't want the end result to look like one part Volkswagen, one part Rolls Royce, and two parts junk heap.

How successful were we? Well, during our first winter in the house, we got a visit from an insurance appraiser. He didn't knock on the door, but examined the exterior of the primed but not yet painted house, measured its perimeter, and took a couple of photographs for his report. We knew nothing of his visit until our insurance agent, an old and valued friend, called. He was laughing.

"Just got your appraisal," he said. "Let me read it to you. 'Nineteenth-century home, in midst of renovation.'"

Hugh Howard writes for the A & E series, In Search of Palladio, *and is the author of several books, including* House-Dreams: How One Man's Vision Became a Family Home, *from which this is adapted (copyright ©2001 Hugh Howard, Algonquin Press). The new-old home he shares with his wife and daughters is in East Chatham, New York.*

WARM WISHES
Tracy Rae Hellerud

My family had lived for generations in a small town on the edge of the Red River Valley of eastern North Dakota. All of my friends could name their first, second, third and fourth cousins. We were a close-knit community, bred from strong people. I loved my family, but even as a child I had dreams that extended past the county and state lines that bordered so many of the dreams of my friends. I wanted sunshine, *warm* sunshine that lasted more than a couple of months each year. And I dreamed of the sea.

One of my favorite pictures in the family albums shows the swing set in our back yard, a typical metal contraption with a basket swing, two chain swings, and a slide on one end with me at the top, smiling wide. A plastic kiddie pool bulges with water at the bottom of the picture. When I was a little older, I was driven with other kids from our small town to swimming lessons at the nearest public pool, 30 miles away. Then, as teens, we gathered at local dams to swim and lie in the sun.

Summer was also the time to lie in the thick, green grass on my grandparents' farm and watch the clouds float by. But every year, fall's chill winds blasted away the heat I loved with bitter promise of much worse to come. The family photos of winter show me frowning and pouting. I remember being uncomfortable in the thick coats, snow pants, gloves, boots, caps and scarves. I didn't enjoy the snow sports that everyone else did. I was wet and tired long before the other kids were ready to give up their toboggans and snow forts. Whatever else North Dakota winters are, they are *long;* they held little redeeming pleasure for me.

My grandma relates a favorite family story of a beautiful snowy day when I was small. She called me to the window to see the pretty snowflakes that most children love. When I saw them, I threw my doll on the floor and began to cry.

As the years passed, Grandpa farmed in the summer, but he and Grandma fled North Dakota before winter for south Texas. Postcards from Tropic Star RV Park, near McAllen, arrived from Grandma, displaying rows of palm trees. Grandma called with talk of picking oranges right off the trees, traveling across the border to shop for trinkets in Mexico, and taking an hour's drive to the coast to collect seashells. I watched the weather news on television most nights and could see that south Texas had a lot of the country's high temperatures during our long, cold winters.

By the time I was in college, the strong feelings I had about the seasons had intensified. At the University of North Dakota campus, I walked in the snow and 40-below-zero weather to get to class. Gazing into fireplaces and bonfires, I longed for a warmer locale.

When I traveled with a friend to visit his family in Florida, I was entranced with the tropical landscape, the small lizards darting in the shrubbery, and the warm air that stayed with us, even at night. Lying in the sun on Bradenton beach, I was mesmerized by the waves, salt air and the sound of the seagulls. Looking out onto that beautiful Gulf water, I made a vow, "I don't know exactly where, but someday I will live near that water!"

I returned to North Dakota with an intense desire to go south, but I had work to do. I completed my nursing degree and decided to take my first nursing job in a hospital in Fargo. I wanted to stay close to family until I had some experience to add to a resume. I drove through blizzards and on ice, and I kept the hope that someday the chill in my bones would be warmed away. I studied brochures and travel books. I sent for applications for hospitals in Texas, California and Hawaii. I read and reread the enticements of the average number of days of sunshine. Fargo, North

Dakota, had an average of 88 sunny days; McAllen, Texas, boasted 280. Reading about the all-year flowers and sea breezes in the "Tropical Tip of Texas," my heart began to beat a little faster.

But I still didn't know where I would start my new life. I traveled to California but I was too much a small-town girl to imagine myself fitting into a California lifestyle. I found Hawaii attractive, but its cost of living didn't seem manageable on a nurse's salary. My grandparents had been traveling to Texas for 15 years by this time, so I decided a trip to visit them would give me a chance to see if the Texas they adored, and the one so enticingly described in promotional literature, was for me. I began, and quickly ended, my search for a new home during a February visit to the Rio Grande Valley. In nine days, I'd fallen in love with the warmth of the sun, water, and people on the border. There were palm trees, bougainvillea, fresh fruits and short winters.

I applied for positions at two of the local hospitals and was offered a job as a nurse in intensive care at one of them. At 7:30 on the last morning of my vacation, I lay under a palm tree, breathing in the warmth of 70 degrees. When I landed that evening in Fargo, the temperature was minus eight. I couldn't wait to get back to Texas and let my new, warm life begin.

Within two weeks of my return to North Dakota, I began packing, although my departure date was months away. On my car visor I placed a small bear in a Hawaiian shirt and a straw hat, with the logo "Life's a Beach,"—a reminder, as my front-wheel-drive car plowed through Fargo's snow drifts, that I would soon be heading south. A late spring snowstorm that year was nearly unbearable. I grumbled and retrieved thick hunting gloves to shovel away the wet snow blocking my garage entrance. Finally, in my apartment, I attempted to make a cup of hot chocolate, but my cold fingers were too stiff to hold the spoon to stir. I would've cried if I hadn't known I'd soon be heading south.

Over the Fourth of July weekend in 1989, I bid North Dakota friends good-bye and waved to the mover as my furniture left town in his truck. I drove from Fargo with my car loaded down with my most valuable possessions, including those childhood photos of summer.

Three days later, I arrived in McAllen, my cold past 1,600 miles behind me. I was homesick some those first few days in a motel—after all, Fargo in July is a happy place. But pretty soon, I was part of south Texas life at the hospital, and I'd made new friends in my new apartment complex, where the swimming pool beckoned all year long.

On a trip to North Dakota the next year to visit my family, I was reunited with an old friend who soon joined me in Texas and became my husband. We moved to a condo on the bay of the Laguna Madre, just ten minutes from the Gulf.

The spell of Texas has never lifted. It eventually lured my brother and his family and my parents to the state, and even my grandparents resigned their snowbird status to live here fulltime.

Now my husband and I live in Lockhart, in central Texas, complete with bluebonnets and a quaint town square. Just yesterday, my mother-in-law called from North Dakota to let us know it was snowing in April. My husband and I had just come in from a dip in the pool when her call came. This weekend, we may drive to the beach, a half-day away. I'm overjoyed to live in the place, where I've always belonged. I am home. And I am warm.

Tracy Rae Hellerud, a member of the Texas Writer's League, has had work published in the Country Extra.

FIRE IN THE VALLEY
Elizabeth Testa

A single thunderhead. I stare. It has been weeks since rain fell, and none is predicted now. This cloud is dazzling. Billowing upwards against an impeccable cobalt sky, layers heaped upon layers like marshmallow fluff, the cloud seems made more of solid substance than of mist.

A grasshopper collides with my leg; it is one of a battalion. In this year of extreme drought, lonely blades of anemic grass struggle valiantly against the insects in our chalky tan pasture. I pluck at my shirt, heat-glued to my chest. The thunderhead is an unexpected gift. As if to wring it out, my empty fingers squeeze and release. I call for my husband to come outside; he will relish this, too, especially since he's been promising—however unscientifically—the rain would come. But while I wait for him, I see ominous details: This cloud swells from an amber underside, and is blowing northeast—toward us and too fast. Not moisture. Wildfire, and from the size of the cloud, an enormous one.

My husband and I climb the 50-foot hill behind the house, Pete at first in confident denial. It's nearly sunset, he says, you're seeing the reflection. He wants rain so badly he teases me about paranoia, as though joking could settle the question in our favor. But watching the cloud from the hilltop, we both swallow further argument.

We decide to drive to a higher vantage point. The broad vista leaves no doubt. Roiling boulders of smoke—charcoal, pink, orange—chase upwards from the ridge opposite ours. Our signal cloud is merged with many, all advancing along the far crest. Fluffy? No. These clouds are the menacing companions of a ravenous fire.

Even from this high, it's hard to gauge distance in the Rockies, but it's comforting to see no actual flames. Pete's hand unclenches from the steering wheel. I take a sip of bottled water. It's in the national forest, must be ten miles, he assures me. No homes over there. No one in danger.

I think of the dense, beautiful stands of oak I've ridden through on horseback, the thick groves of pine. A hundred years overdue, muses my husband, who knows fire is nature's way of cleansing thick forest. He appears not to worry about the fire. They'll put it out before it gets too big, he says, didn't they save the Edgemont subdivision just last week?

I nod, mesmerized by the smoke.

We turn on the radio: At 2:30 that afternoon a passerby spotted a fire on a switchback north of Durango, Colorado. By 5:00, we're told, the blaze has consumed 200 acres, feeding avidly on brittle scrub and bleached grasses. High winds gave the flames a booster ride up the steep slope. Two hours later, 1,500 acres have burned. As we listen and watch, close to sunset, we hear that 2,200 acres are now ash.

The Monday morning news increases the tally to 5,000 acres. Homes near the origin are evacuated, but none in our valley. The day feels almost normal, but I put off two appointments to stay home. Worry and fear do battle with excitement. The dark clouds are terrible and beautiful at the same time. Hourly, I check the sky and ridgelines for flames; it's impossible to believe that so much smoke could come from so many miles away.

The house begins to smell. I remind myself we got smoke from even more distant burns, from Black Ridge at 20 miles, Mesa Verde at 60. In the late afternoon, I can't resist another trip to the high spot. The line of smoke along the opposite ridge has tripled. I fail to describe the scene adequately to Pete, who is changing the tractor oil. "It has?" He looks up. "Want to help me get the horses in for their grain?"

Tuesday brings more of the same, a shocking 20,000-acre

count, and the information that the fire is traveling our way. I postpone more appointments and tether myself to the radio; even repeat bulletins comfort with their lack of fresh news. It's better than hearing something new and scary.

Pete relies on me for updates while he goes about his daily routine: working at the computer, harrowing the field, cleaning up after the horses. I vacillate—he is either braver or more foolhardy than I. He is serene. He makes jokes. Has he not noticed?

I begin to acquire the firefighting jargon, which heightens my sense of the fire's enormity. A Type II Fire Management Team arrives to replace our exhausted volunteers. There is talk of slurry bombers, helicopters and smokejumpers. Crews dig hand lines and call for "dozer assistance," and the fire lines are now measured not in feet but in miles. To help our overworked Colorado teams, firemen from places like Idaho and Montana are flown in, and the county's endangered areas are divided into zones. No more quaint local names—instead of Sweetwater Springs, our farm is part of Zone Charlie-Zebra. I align the fire's direction with the alphabet, and find scant comfort in being in a C, even if the appended letter is Z. By our inclusion, I realize we are not simply spectators.

Containment statistics are grim; without rain, the crews have little chance of extinguishing the flames. Where will we get enough water to put out the blaze? And when?

"When it snows," answers the county emergency management director. Everyone does the math: six months 'til winter, more than a million acres of fuel in the Weminuche wilderness. When the wind shifts there's a collective epiphany: No Hadrian's Wall separates private land from the Weminuche, just ink on a government map. Neighbors begin to clear decades of overgrown scrub. Conversations are salted with discussion of ladder fuels and defensible space. Chainsaw use is banned, but the local

True Value sells out of handsaws and lopping shears. Even the most derelict dump truck is jump-started into service.

I look out our home-office window at three acres of thick brush. Pete tells me not to worry; it's an island of oak with pasture around it. I think about Charlie-Zebra.

According to the Fire Behavior Specialist, we are at the mercy of the fire's distinct personality: this one is lively at sunset and after, but "lays down" in the early mornings, acting like a controlled burn. Cooler night air eventually sucks the flames to ground level, but the trade-off for weakened fire activity is the influx of choking, greasy smoke. It invades everywhere, in the kitchen drawers, under the bed sheets. Across our pasture Wednesday morning, the distant pines are masked in a cool blue-gray and we can't make out more than the outline of a neighbor's pond. When a heron flaps up from the water, the horses startle and run; they can't see any better than we can. The sky is skim-milk white, the sunlight a dull, heavily filtered orange, as artificial looking as stage lighting.

I make a videotape of the house. As I sweep each room's contents into the camera, I feel silly. Pete says it's a good idea, but it seems he's sure we won't need it. We talk about what we would take, the implications of "if" hovering unspoken between us. We decide we'd pack almost nothing—it's all insured, I think, and I won't want to be slowed down. Pete's just thinking the place won't burn. I monitor the sky so often my neck cramps, and I pack boxes with an emergency office: phonebook, calendar, the laptop. I put it all in the car; Pete laughs and again I wonder if I'm overreacting. No one near us is being told to leave, and although we are bathed in grit and ash and chunks of singed bark, we can still see no actual fire from our house.

In the afternoons, the wind clears the air and also kicks the flames into hyperdrive. Exploding trees send debris into giant plumes of heat and embers, which eventually collapse and scatter the blazing material for miles. Monday, Tuesday, now Wednesday—every day the fire makes huge advances this way.

A neighbor comes by. While we confer about ponds and pumps, an aspen leaf drifts down between us, landing on the gravel by his ATV tire. I pick it up; the size of my smallest fingernail, it must have come from a tree just budding out—early June is barely spring in the high country where the fire rages. Perfectly formed but blackened through, the delicate leaf disintegrates in my hand.

Thursday morning, I wake up dizzy with the craving for oxygen. The deck is speckled with thousands of tiny crescents, like eyelashes heavy with mascara: burnt pine needles. At the mailbox, I find a partially charred pinecone; when I pick it up, I see a circle of ash beneath. I confirm a room for us with friends at safe distance. Probably weary of my badgering, Pete agrees it's time to move the horses to safer ground, which I do, in smoke so thick any approaching high beams look like penlights.

The daily plume builds to a tower thousands of feet high; it begins to lean over us. Neighbors call, and Pete helps them get their livestock out. Meanwhile, I pile clothes willy-nilly into my bag. One day? Five? Forever? Every time I touch something, my fingertips say good-bye. Ashamed of the melodrama, or wanting to disbelieve, I change good-bye to maybe.

The subdivision a mile away is put on pre-evacuation status; from there the fire could have an easy trip through heavy fuel load to our area. A secret voice I want to silence insists on baiting the fire: Just try it, the voice taunts, let's get this battle over with. I want to watch fire crews put out the flames; then I will feel safe.

Between trips with animals, Pete loads our truck: the Navajo rugs, boxes of family photographs, a case of wine. At some point, he packs a small duffel for himself. I notice he only includes two

HOPE IS THE THING WITH FEATHERS

Hope is the thing with feathers
That perches in the soul,
And sings the tune without all the words,
And never stops at all.
And sweetest in the gale is heard;
And sore must be the storm
That could abash the little bird
That kept so many warm.

I've heard it in the chillest land,
And on the strangest sea;
Yet, never in extremity.
It asked a crumb of me.

—Emily Dickinson

days' worth of underwear. I can't decide what that means.

At 7:30, the calls come, five within five minutes. I swallow hard as three friends with scanners tell me the fire is rolling through an adjacent tract. One of them uses the term "firestorm."

Two neighbors report flames are visible now from their places. "The treetops are flying off like tornadoes," the one with binoculars says.

I think, what should I do? But I am paralyzed with shock.

Pete finds me standing beside the Jeep. The only thing I can do is toss car keys from hand to hand. "We have to go now," I say. "*Now!*"

Pete looks at me. "Let's take more of the paintings," he says. "We've got time."

"Please, let's just go," I beg. "Now."

One object at a time, Pete gets me to focus. Passing through the garage, I remember the dogs' leashes. Pete throws in his favorite cowboy boots; I add an old photograph of my father. Minute by minute, even as I scan the sky, I calm down. By 10:30 we are done. The house does not look empty, yet it echoes. I whistle the dogs to the jeep.

"Well, McGee?" Pete asks with a quick kiss and a smile, the truck door ajar. His eyelids droop, a sure sign he's exhausted. "It's been a great place to live." We turn together to gaze at the house.

How lovely it is, the warm light beckoning from inside, brightening the poppies in the front garden. The tranquility belies the encroaching fire. I try not to cry.

Pete squeezes my shoulder and whispers, "Would you think less of me if I told you I've already planned the replacement?"

At that precise moment, as I tip my head back to laugh, I know I am leaving with my most precious possession. It is amazing to think that we can start over with just the two of us, but it is true.

The photos and clothes in the back seat are just a bonus. Everything will be fine. The fire is suddenly an adventure, and we will survive. If the house burns down—and in the end it didn't— I won't have lost my home. But laughing in the jeep that night, while my husband tells me that it might be a chance for some "home improvements," I feel safe and happy. And I still do.

Nowadays, I am sure rain will eventually come and the lakes will fill, as sure as I am of loving this man for the rest of my days. His optimism is the roof over my head.

Elizabeth Testa, co-editor of JUSTICE: True Stories of Fair Play, *lives near Durango, Colorado. When not editing, she trains horses.*

SECTION V

◆ Potpourri of Wishes ◆

"Hope is the pillar that holds up the world."
—Pliny

THE BLUE GARDEN
Sylvia Halliday

What caught our attention first was the single azure crocus, half-hidden in the snow, pushing its insistent way under a broad plank fence.

Pat and I were freshmen together that long ago time in Providence, Rhode Island. College Hill, overlooking a then-unremarkable and drab city, was a wonder of magnificent old turn-of-the-century mansions. The school had bought some half dozen or so of these old houses, scattered on side streets, and turned them into Freshmen Houses for the newcomers, providing a cozier environment to ease our transition into college than the large and impersonal women's dorms located on campus.

But Pat and I didn't fit in anyway. We were the socially inept, timid dreamers, the romantics, the oddballs—all well and good in high school, when you could go home to a family that understood you, but isolating in college, where being popular and dating a lot carried so much weight. We ached to fit in with the "regular" crowd, wishing we had more in common with them.

So we "hung out" together, or whatever the terminology was in those days, building a tentative and shy friendship, which helped to fend off the feelings of despair and helplessness that lurked behind every social snub, overbearing professor or shaky grade. More than once, we had bolstered each other when the urge came to admit defeat and just go home.

It was a gloomy March day when we saw the crocus. The remnants of the recent snowfall—little soot-and-mud-stained patches—covered the sidewalk in front of the high fence, which seemed to run completely around its lot. We usually avoided walking back to our dorm on this side of the street, particularly in bad weather: The decrepit old fence and the untended side-

walk—soggy leaves in the fall and icy patches in winter—had always seemed unfriendly. Moreover, the box-like '30s apartment houses on either side of the lot held no interest for us, compared to the glories of the Victorian houses.

But that spot of blue-purple, glowing even in the gray afternoon light, had caught our eye. We marveled at the tenacity of the little flower, defying both the weather and the forbidding fence. Curious now, we strained to see through the cracks in the fence, but in vain. Undeterred, Pat searched and found a loose plank near the corner of the lot and, despite my feeble protests (she was always bolder than I), managed to pry it loose. We felt like sneak thieves as we wedged ourselves through the opening.

The lot we were in was probably no more than 20 by 30 feet—a wild, overgrown space that had clearly once been a garden, attached to a long-razed house. There were several bare trees, patches of unkempt bushes and shrubs, even a few gravel paths, peeping from a covering of pristine snow that held not a single footprint. In the center of the garden were two semicircular stone benches, stained and crumbling, and a large trellis, with thick, knotted tendrils of some sort of vine twisting through its wrought-iron curlicues. The crocuses were everywhere, gleaming like sapphires and amethysts on a gossamer white quilt.

We stood transfixed, feeling as though we had stumbled upon a magical land, a place where no one had ever been before. We giggled like children sharing a delicious secret, etched our names in the crusted snow, and vowed to return again.

Pat pointed to the vine. "I'll bet it's grapes," she said. "But we'll have to wait till next fall to see."

We visited our secret garden regularly that spring. We watched purple iris come up, saw violets twinkling in the overgrown grass, held our breaths in anticipation in the weeks before the lilac trees burst into fragrant bloom. Going out for coffee before curfew, we would duck into the garden and sit on the benches in the scented night, pouring out our hearts to each other.

We shared our offbeat pleasures—my interest in antique hats and fans, Pat's love of old folksongs (I still remember her particularly lachrymose rendition of "Queen Jane Lay in Labor.") We even invented fanciful tales of the Victorian lady who had created this magical space, picturing her strolling in her garden on a spring evening, dressed in white linen. Lost in our secret world, we felt safe, untouched, and mysteriously connected to the past. Somehow, that kinship made it easier to look to our unknown futures with more confidence and hope. Life was a continuum, an unending progression of good times and bad, and our petty concerns were miniscule streams when measured against the vast river of the human condition.

It was just at the end of our freshman year that the garden unfolded its final secret for us. In the rush of final exams and packing and leave-taking, we had not been back for weeks. And perhaps, having survived that first difficult year, we thought that the garden had helped us through, but now that we were about to return home, we no longer needed its shelter. But, on the last day of school, Pat and I agreed to visit the garden and exchange farewell gifts there.

We pulled aside the old plank, as usual, stepped through, and gasped in unison. Indifferent to our neglect, the garden had continued to grow. The ragged bushes now held the buds of blue hydrangeas, and veronicas and delphinium thrust their azure spikes toward the sun. And the vine, green and flowering, proved to be wisteria, its heavy clusters of sweet-scented lavender blossoms festooning the arbor in breathtaking swags of color.

Pat turned to me, her eyes filling with tears. "It's a *blue* garden," she whispered. "There's not another color here!" And surely it was so—not a single red or yellow rosebush, so beloved by the Victorians, not one pink peony to mar the perfection.

We hugged each other and murmured our thanks to the long-ago lady who had had such an offbeat and original idea. *She* hadn't been afraid to be different, to follow her own star, to nourish her vision, no matter how far from "conventional wisdom" it might place her.

Bolstered by that symbol of uniqueness when I came back to college, I found the courage to reach out for friendships, no matter how unconventional; to unashamedly join the "weird" theater group; to transform myself into the person I *wanted* to be, not the person I *thought* I should be. Pat stopped worrying about being an "egghead" (our term for "nerd"), buried herself in her beloved books and took on a double major. She graduated Phi Beta Kappa.

I married in June of my senior year—a fellow Brown student. My bridal bouquet was a huge armful of blue delphinium, casually arranged (over the florist's objections) to look as though I had just picked them from "my" blue garden.

I lost touch with Pat through the years, and the lot was cleared in the '60s to make room for a cramped and ugly little modern house. But I still visit the street when I go back for reunions, and remember Pat and our magical, mysterious, wonderful Blue Garden. And I give thanks to the unknown Victorian lady, whose singular dream gave us so much strength and hope, and faith in our uniqueness.

Sylvia Halliday is the editor of WISDOM: True Stories of Life's Lessons. *She also has 14 published novels to her credit and can't wait until her six grandchildren get old enough to read them. She lives in Forest Hills, New York.*

MORNING PROMISE
Paula Timpson

Pink skies sing new hope

The doe of the morning light

Gives us inner joy

Paula Timpson is the author of two verse volumes, The Spirit of Hiking in the Hamptons *and* Poetry for the Soul, *published by iuniverse.com. She lives in East Hampton, New York.*

LIKE MINDS?

"If you had one word to speak to the world, what would that word be?"
                                                    —Frank Sinatra

"That word would be hope."   —Eleanor Roosevelt

NOT JUST ANOTHER MOOSE
Colleen Madonna Flood Williams

She was an old cow. Her hide was scarred, and she moved with the assurance of the mature. She knew where she was, and where she was going. It was time for this moose to calve and she was going to do it in our backyard.

Having just moved into this house in Alaska, we were unprepared for this guest. She, however, was prepared to do what she had traveled to our yard to do: give birth. She did not seem to care one bit that we might believe that she was in *our* yard. This was *her* birthing area and, in her eyes, we were the trespassers.

For the next five years, my son and I were blessed with the opportunity of watching this mother calve. She almost always produced a pair of gangly chestnut red twins, and invariably lost one of those twins over the course of the long Kenai winter. Although I didn't think she ever took much notice of me, I often wondered if she knew I was ill, and how much watching her lifted my spirits.

She was something to ruminate upon as I underwent ten months of surgery, chemotherapy and radiation for breast cancer at Roswell Park Cancer Institute in Buffalo, New York. I would wonder if she missed me peering out of my back windows to watch her. I would hope that she was all right, and that she would still be around if, and when, I made it back home.

I asked my husband to keep an eye out for her. My son, Paul, spent a great deal of time with me in Buffalo, so he didn't see the moose much that winter.

She was nowhere to be found when I arrived home with a clean bill of health. Something in me knew that she was gone. Perhaps old age, a motorist, a disease or a predator had brought her down. I didn't know what had happened to her. I only knew that she was gone.

I wept, thinking of the new gangly calves that I had so looked forward to seeing in my backyard. I was back here and healthy—it wasn't fair that my special friend was gone.

About a month after I'd returned, I discovered that there was another, younger cow nosing about the brushy areas of my backyard. I told myself that this was one of my friend's daughters, come home to give birth in the same place that she had been born. I spied an anxious yearling observing her from the neighboring trees.

I smiled at my son. Another mother moose had come to visit our yard; I was sure that she would become *our* mother moose. We would watch her, worry about her and feel affection for her, just as we had for her predecessor.

I closed my eyes and pictured the grandchildren that my son might someday give me. I hoped he would bring his future wife to the still half-wild place where he'd been raised when she was ready to give birth. I wished them the luck of being able to look out their back window and watch a mother moose of their own, nudging her chestnut red calves onto their feet for the very first time.

That first mother moose, and the more recent birthing moose I believe is her offspring, have been my teachers. Why? Well, they taught me about the circle of life.

The old moose cow also taught me that it is not how long we have upon this earth but how many lives we touch that really matters. I learned, too, that we can affect someone's life without ever realizing it.

And, don't laugh, but because of that cow, I believe in moose heaven. I know she is there somewhere. I picture her grazing contentedly as a warm summer breeze keeps the mosquitoes off of her back. The image brings me great peace and joy.

Colleen Madonna Flood Williams and her moose live in Homer, Alaska.

HOPE

Art Goodtimes

for Buzz & Jean Zatterstrom

bent but undeterred

the elder spruce

along Leopard Creek

on the grade up to

the ghost towns of Sams & Noel

stands sturdy

the wind has done

all it can

the crushing snows

but nature knows

nothing can stop

the heartwood's green fuse

from rising

like flame & bursting

into needles

Art Goodtimes of Telluride, Colorado, is an elected Green Party politician and an organic farmer specializing in heirloom seed potatoes.

MAN'S BEST FRIEND
Robin Pritts

O ne late Monday evening in September, I intended to take my dog, Shelton, out for a nice long walk. Shelton, whom I'd owned for two wonderful years, is a Bricone frise, a charming poodle mix with big floppy ears and a thick, white coat.

He still had the awkwardness of youth as he clumsily struggled with his big paws, yet whenever I looked into his eyes I felt they were those of a mystic, someone old and wise. On our walk that evening, I stopped to deposit the weekend's accumulated trash in a nearby dumpster.

After making sure that my garbage bag was in the dumpster, I turned around—just in time to avoid being run over by a pickup truck speeding through the condominium's parking lot. Unfortunately, Shelton was not so lucky. I saw his leash disappear under the truck's front tires.

Fortunately, the leash broke, but the panicked Shelton ran off out of sight. I had no idea how far his adrenaline-fueled legs would carry him, but my guess was too far for me to find him on my own. I called my family and friends, and we all began to search high and low for poor Shelton. But he'd disappeared into the dark September evening, and I was finally forced to go home—*without* Shelton.

Over the next few days, I was lost without my dog. I realized how important my best friend had been to me, and I resolved to continue the search. My sister, Janice, drove 150 miles to come help me find Shelton. Day after day, we searched the surrounding area, trying to catch a glimpse of him. I posted flyers with Shelton's picture, the date he had been lost, and my phone number everywhere I could think of, but each day I returned to my apartment to find the answering machine

CHARMED CRAFT

Charm quilts were a charming trend of the late 19th century—the fad seemed to take hold in about 1870 and flourished for a good 30 years. What distinguished these handmade quilts from others is that no two patches, or not more than two patches, in any one quilt were the same.

Certainly, these quilts, like most ones of old, served the triple purposes of using up fabric scraps and layering beds in warmth, while also offering hours of social companionship to their industrious female makers. But why the stricture against using more than one or two bits of the same cloth?

Historians of craft are unsure about this, but I like to think that the inspiration behind the charm quilt was not merely frivolous. Rather, the making of one prompted each contributor to reflect a moment on the uniqueness of what she had to offer. I like to believe that she chose each cloth piece she would stitch into the whole, musing on what she had earlier crafted of the same fabric and why. To me, the charm quilt is intricately linked with both household and community memories—that is, with earlier hopes and their fruition.

There also seems a connection of sorts between charm quilts and the roughly contemporaneous fad of button charm strings made by girls and young women. To make a button string, an unmarried female, most often a teenager, collected unmatched buttons. Her goal was to string together 999 buttons before she was married, then add one more after her wedding day. Clearly, embarking on a button string spoke of matrimonial hope—but perhaps not too soon. Collecting for the strings seems to have been mostly a game—in the spirit that future youngsters would collect and trade baseball or other character cards, or even Absolut ads. But I imagine a long button string as an informal part of a young lady's trousseau, promising her a lifetime source for missing odd buttons. Either that, or she eventually broke up her collection, contributing buttons from it to younger hopefuls.

Some charm quilts were also fashioned on a 999-parts

(continued on next page)

rule—very large quilts, however, might incorporate even more snips of cloth. Charm quilt patterns are notable for their use of a mosaic or hexagon pattern, as well as equilateral, isosceles and half-square triangles. Quilters would arrange the hexagonal patches in rosettes, starting in the middle of the quilt and then moving outward in ever increasing rings. The hexagons would be joined together at their corners by triangles, creating a delightful pattern.

Each woman who stitched together the scraps would have had to trade fabric leftovers with yet more relatives and friends, to ensure scrap bags varied enough in color and pattern selection to embark on a charm quilt. The making of the quilt was often accompanied by games that young and old alike enjoyed. Challenges spun out to remember what else had also been made—and where, when and by whom—from the parent bolt of each scrap. Informal contests were held to find the matching cloth piece in the quilt itself, an ancestor of the "Memory" card game today's young children play.

Making a charm quilt appears to have been a lot of fun. Small wonder, then, that this type of quilt, even more than other quilts, is a memory quilt, and as such some have survived as treasured family heirlooms.

Charm quilts became popular again in the 1930s and early 1940s—an era of enforced economizing and, during the war, female home-front togetherness. The making of these quilts has become popular today. Charm quilters, I believe, are drawn to this craft challenge because of its artistic and social value.

empty of messages concerning his whereabouts.

We continued looking for him. If I couldn't see Shelton, then perhaps he would see or smell me, and come running up. But that didn't happen. On the weekend, my parents came to visit and join the search.

I missed everything about Shelton: his comforting, silent company; his warm, furry paws; his good-natured barks each night when I returned home, weary from work. My mood was dark. I had lost a true friend, whether he walked on two legs—or four. It didn't matter to me; a friend is a friend.

I could not accept that Shelton was gone forever. Somewhere, he was alive and desperately waiting to be found by his master.

As the somber weekend drew to a close and my family prepared to leave, they tried to make me accept that Shelton would not be coming home. To get my mind off my loss, my parents, my sister, and my future brother-in-law took me out for dinner and were planning on going to a movie afterward. Despite myself, I enjoyed the good food and warm company.

Still . . . Shelton was gone. I insisted on calling home after dinner to check my answer-phone messages. Just in case.

And there was a message there! A man said he had spotted a dog matching Shelton's description in the bushes not far from where I'd lost him. The caller somehow felt that the dog would still be there—*if* I hurried.

My family and I raced to the condo parking lot in my dad's SUV and screeched to a halt. No sooner had I opened the car door than I heard Shelton's whimpering from inside a thick wall of sheltering bushes.

Shelton responded to my voice and emerged looking no worse for the wear. In fact, he had somehow managed to gain weight in the week we had been apart.

Robin Pritts of Aurora, Illinois, is the author of From CP to CPA: One Man's Triumph over the Disability of Cerebral Palsy.

EUROPE OR BUST

B. B. Jones

When my sister Sara told me she was going with me to Europe, I nearly laughed. Not that it was funny, really. She wanted to go more than anything, and I loved the idea of having her travel with me. But it was such an outlandish thing for her to say. The thing was, I considered her a petulant little princess who, up until three months before, had never held a real job and who, to the best of my knowledge, could not have had more than ten dollars in her bank account. A silver-spoon baby whose only concern had been to get good grades, she had just begun to learn how to pay her own way—barely—in a big city. And now it seemed as if she had gone completely off the deep end.

Sara and I are the daughters of upper-middle class parents in Sonoma County—California's wine country, which has often ranked among America's most desirable places to live. Riding to school in our mother's Mercedes station wagon, Sara never had any doubts about her future. Her plan was simple: high school, then USC (University of Southern California) or maybe UC Santa Cruz. Perhaps a year of schooling in France or England would follow; then she would settle down to a respectable profession, with someone opening those career doors for her. It was the path that nearly everyone in our extended family had chosen, and the path that her friends were planning.

It was not, however, the route that I had taken nor, as it turned out, the one that she would take. Our father happened to be of the opinion that a child magically turned into an adult at age sixteen. When I was in my senior year of high school, I was unceremoniously given the heave-ho from the feathered nest— and two years later, the exact same thing happened to my younger sister. Both of us worked after-school jobs and rented rooms from friends while finishing high school. By Sara's graduation, I had moved to San Francisco. My sister accepted my invitation to join me in my tiny apartment and start searching for a job at one of the city's new dot-com firms.

As her friends were preparing to make the leap from home to university, Sara was trying to make the transition from coffee shop counter-girl to office receptionist. Our flat was smaller than some hotel rooms; fast food was a luxury in those days. I was used to some deprivation, but she was not.

As more time passed, the less she liked the pinched life. USC was as unattainable as Never-Never Land. Her life consisted of a nine-hour day answering phones at an accounting firm, followed by a few hours of classes at the city college. Her friends were going to New York, to Mexico, to Boston, to Spain. And Sara? She was stuck.

On my 21st birthday, I received a round-trip ticket to Europe from my godmother. Sara announced matter-of-factly that she would be going as well. I had no idea how I was going to save enough money for lodging and food for myself in Europe. The salary I was making as an office assistant was enough to cover my essential living expenses but almost nothing was left over each month. Sara might want to tag along but she had no idea of the cost. High-season round trip airfare to London? A Eurail pass? Meals? Hotels? Not a chance.

I guess I didn't understand how important going to Europe was for Sara. It wasn't just a vacation, but a necessary milestone, *the* experience that distinguished people who had "gone somewhere and done something" from the people who had failed. It didn't matter that her friends who'd crossed the Atlantic had done so on their parents' dime. Coming with me to Europe became her dream, her most important immediate goal in life.

Was it unrealistic? Of course. Would waiting a couple of years have meant she was a failure? No way. But Sara didn't see it like that.

In the nine months that followed my birthday, Sara seemed to mature ten years, although I didn't then fully acknowledge the change. Focused on my new daily grind—a front desk job at a graphic design agency, and an agent's assistant position at a modeling agency—I only fleetingly paid attention to my sister. In my struggle to achieve and earn more, I was tired all the time.

Sara, on the other hand, appeared to have endless energy. Not that I saw much of her. She was doing double duty at a technical support call center and at the Kaiser library, while picking up weekend shifts at a restaurant and continuing her junior college classes. I did observe that her wardrobe suddenly seemed to be completely composed of khaki pants, black slacks and sensibly tailored shirts—the office casual uniform. Her phone voice, I realized one day, had become patient and perfectly modulated. And I could see that the circles under her eyes had become darker. An acquaintance startled me by guessing her to be about 30 years old. She was barely nineteen.

But her bank account was growing. I had to take notice when she triumphantly announced her savings had hit the thousand-dollar mark. There was no time, really, for long, sisterly conversations. After my alarm went off at six a.m., I'd roll out of bed with a grimace. Almost invariably, Sara had already gone for the day. Occasionally, we would see each other around midnight and exchange a few words over our respective Cup-o-Noodles before staggering off to bed. One night, Sara confided with grim satisfaction that she liked working at the restaurant because she could get a decent meal there and not spend the $2 or so that it cost to buy our instant noodle dinners.

By springtime, I recognized that Sara and I would be making

this European trip together, come summer. It was a stormy, utterly dismal spring that year. No way did my umbrella spare me getting drenched, walking the mile or so between the subway and the apartment. But late at night, huddled up in a comforter, Sara and I discussed the merits of various Riviera towns. We basked in dreams of sunny beaches and gelato and beautiful Frenchmen. In May, I splurged and bought *Frommer's Guide to Europe On Less than $50 Per Day*. It was a big expense, but well worth it. We used it to map out our trip.

I had stopped thinking about Sara's bank account and had started worrying more about my own. Both of us could rattle off our balances down to the penny—and did, often. It was our Number Two topic of conversation, right behind airfare. Sara was compulsive about airfare. She was searching high and low for the best deal. Travel agencies, consolidators, websites—she left no stone unturned. Eventually my godmother found her a sweet deal, which she booked immediately. Not only did I know by then that Sara would have money to spare for other expenses of the trip, I also realized that she had gained the confidence to really enjoy it.

The moment that really stands out, however, the moment that made the trip absolutely real to me, was when together we bought our Eurail passes. The passes, which would give us two months of unlimited train travel throughout a dozen countries, came to about $650 dollars apiece. It was the most that either of us had ever spent on any one thing. I think we both half-expected a bolt of lightning to come out of the sky and knock the pens out of our hands before we could sign the sales slips. When the transaction was completed, we blundered out of the travel agency, giddy.

A few days later, we were on the plane. We snoozed our way from San Francisco to London's Heathrow Airport, leaning our heads on each other's shoulders. We propped our feet on carry-ons that

were filled with film, journals, flimsy bikinis, and CD Walkmans. We each had our precious Eurail passes, passports, pound notes, traveler's checks and 20 crisp one-dollar bills, stashed safely away in little bags hidden under our clothes.

Somehow, no matter how much you sleep on plane flights, you're always drowsy when you disembark—but we didn't care. We were in Europe! We charged through Heathrow at seven in the morning, London time, and navigated the Underground with ease before jubilantly throwing our luggage into the tiny, rose-colored room at a B&B in Chelsea, just a few minutes' walking distance from shops and pubs and . . . oh everything. We laughed hysterically over being served tomatoes and baked beans for breakfast and gaped at the perfectly manicured plants in Kensington Gardens. We ate greasy kebabs for dinner, loving every bite, had a pint in a pub, and went on a ridiculous joyride through the back streets of London with three Italian boys in a Ferrari. And that was all the first day!

We cavorted around Venice with more rowdy Italian boys. We lay on our backs and snapped pictures of the ceiling of the Louvre. We fended off pickpockets in Nice and drank large blue cocktails in Greece. We used those rail passes for all they were worth, going to two dozen cities in six weeks. We ate nothing but gelato for a week straight in Florence and dined on garden snails in Barcelona. We got ridiculously tan.

Sara shot six rolls of film. The pictures are now organized chronologically and neatly labeled in an album that she keeps on her nightstand. Even though each of us has since been back to Europe, and even though each trip no longer represents a financial miracle, or maybe because of those things, our "big trip to Europe" will always be a standout. Once upon a time, I laughed at my sister when she expressed an impossible hope. Now, when Sara says she's going to do something, I believe her.

B.B. Jones is a travel and entertainment writer whose home base is in Los Angeles.

SECTION VI

◆Holiday Hopes◆

"The art of living does not consist in preserving and clinging to a particular mode of happiness, but in allowing happiness to change its form without being disappointed by the change; happiness, like a child, must be allowed to grow up."

—CHARLES L. MORGAN

EASTER TREAT

Bonnie Brayton

I was ten years old, and I was hurt. Here I was, stuck at home for Easter, banned from the family celebration at my grandparents' house. I felt so left out. It just didn't seem to be fair.

My parents tried to tell me that it wasn't anything I had done, but I just couldn't be around Grandpa because I had a sore throat, which might make him sick again. Grandpa Bill had returned home from the hospital just in time for Easter, but he was in fragile health. The left side of his body had become paralyzed after an accident on a construction site some decades ago. He also suffered from diabetes. And his recent illness had left him especially vulnerable to the germs plaguing me. My grandmother, Doreen, just couldn't risk having me in the house.

I knew what the gathering would be like, and I was very upset I wouldn't be there. I liked being in the thick of our warm extended family. All my aunts and uncles and my many cousins, bouncing with energy, would be there. Everyone who counted would be on hand—except me. My cousins would giggle as they were assembled to stroll outside to see the carrot that lay atop a patio chair. That carrot would have a single bite mark in it, *proving* the existence of the Easter bunny.

Then each child would be handed a basket and told the Easter egg hunt would begin in a moment. That announcement would surely be met, as it had in past years, with shrieks of joy. I wanted to be in the yard with my cousins, frantically running around trying to be the one who found the most eggs. The best eggs would be the brightly colored plastic ones; those were the ones containing little treats.

But I was stuck at home. No evidence of a magical bunny. No

hidden eggs. No trove of sweets. No fun.

After the exciting Easter egg hunt, the kids would join the grown-ups at Grandma's long wooden table and get some real food in their tummies. That would be fun, too.

Thinking about what I'd be missing, it seemed to me that almost worse than not laying claim to my share of chocolate was just not being there with my relatives. Some of them I hadn't seen in many months and, even if I didn't understand every single, good-humored story, I would miss the laughter that invariably rang through our big family gatherings. And I'd be cheated out of the moment I always stole with grandfather, sitting on his knee as he told a story about his life. "Grandpa," I'd inevitably ask, "tell me the story of how you got hurt."

And Grandpa would indulge me once more, beginning with his description of the construction site in Tempe, Arizona. If he paused, I could and would fill in the next phrase.

The plan this Easter was that my mother and younger brother would go to my grandparents for brunch, while my father, who also had a sore throat, would stay with me. How could an Easter alone with my dad possibly be as good as the one I'd miss?

My father asked me what I'd like to do with him, and I sullenly informed him that I did not want to do anything. Dad ignored my bad humor and took me out to a favorite deli called Bowman's in Old Town Scottsdale for breakfast. I loved Bowman's and my spirits lifted a little as we walked in. Over breakfast, it was decided that we would go to the gardens at the Scottsdale Civic Center for a walk.

I had been to the Civic Center several times with my elementary school. We'd visited its museum, and once we attended a production of *The Velveteen Rabbit* there, but I'd never spent time in its copious gardens. They were, I had to admit, lovely and included several fountains and grassy fields as well as the plant-

ed portions, which burst with exquisite flowers in a riot of colors.

The flowers, dancing in the slight breezes, seemed to beckon me to be their playmate. Losing the last of my petulance, I darted from blossom to blossom, happily chirping to my father about how pretty they were. And I wasn't disturbing anyone, because that day Dad and I almost had the garden to ourselves.

I ran among pansies, snapdragons, begonias, petunias, roses and violas, occasionally plucking a bloom that I added to a little bouquet that I planned on presenting to my mother later in the day.

My dad and I also talked that morning, which was in itself a rare treat. Rarely did my father get home from work before my bedtime. And, I'm sorry to say, around that time our weekend family activities generally involved arguing. Maybe parent/child "quality time" is something easier prescribed than taken, but on that day my dad and I experienced it. Like one of the flowers in the garden, I opened up to him, telling him about school, and of my worries and desires. In front of a tiered fountain, we also talked about his work and even movies we'd liked.

As I look back, it wasn't so much our conversational topics that were remarkable as my father's tone. He spoke with me not as a parent to a small child, but as if we were two people whose views mattered equally. It was the first of many similar conversations we'd have as I entered and made my way through adolescence toward adulthood. My father always took me seriously in our talks. That is something I value greatly, and which I know started the Easter morning that began with me feeling so left out.

My grandfather died later that year and yes, I'm still a bit sorry I wasn't there for his last Easter. Still, I would not trade that brilliant morning with my father for a hundred Easter egg hunts or a dozen baskets of chocolates. A sore throat kept me from one opportunity but amidst the snapdragons and dancing fountain waters I was given another—a chance for the relationship between my father and me to blossom.

I realize, of course, that neither mode of spending Easter morning is a conventional religious one. But I personally cannot think of a better way to participate in the spirit of rebirth than the way I spent that special Easter morning.

Bonnie Brayton continues to enjoy springtime in Phoenix.

A THANKSGIVING TO REMEMBER
Maryann Ostermeyer

T wo years ago, I transferred to Cajon Valley Middle School, a wonderful school on the floor of the El Cajon Valley, California, to teach students in the Newcomers and English Language Learners program. Taking roll in my new classroom was like trying to twist my mouth into the shape of a pretzel as I dealt with all the unfamiliar names. The children in my class came from 15 different countries.

Wherever there had been political or social strife in the world, those were the places my kids had called home. I learned to pronounce the names belonging to the bright, hopeful faces of children who had fled the tribal wars of Sierra Leone and the Sudan, political unrest in the Middle East, and the Bosnian war. These refugees were thrown together with new immigrants from Latin America. Mine was the first schoolroom some of the kids had ever been in. And many of them had seen things no child or adult should ever see. No one is, or maybe should be, grown up enough to absorb a memory of babies' heads floating in a river.

I wanted to do something to make the children in my class know they were in a new, safe country. We'd enjoyed Halloween together, but the holiday that I really wanted them to appreciate was Thanksgiving. I figured that planning a Thanksgiving dinner for lunchtime would combine teaching them English and a bit of American custom with fun.

I asked the kids whom we should invite to our dinner, surveying them for the names of people they wanted to "thank." We decided to invite the four core teachers who ran the program, as well as the ten college tutors who worked with students in our school. The kids also wanted to invite the 30 "Students Plus" kids in other classes—some of these, of course, were their siblings.

Anyone else? The kids said they were grateful to the school support staff and wanted to invite them, too. This would mean that administrators at both the school and the district office should also get invitations. What about the parents who volunteered so much time to the school? And, of course, we couldn't forget the people at the International Rescue Committee.

Our invitation list grew to over 200 people. Aside from actual family members, each guest had either helped my students come here or helped them adjust to their new surroundings.

While the children threw themselves into making Thanksgiving-party invitations, I looked at my checkbook and cringed. While I was more than happy to help pay for the dinner, I had very little spare cash, due to medical bills for the treatment of serious burns I'd suffered the year before. Money aside, how was I going to cook enough turkey for all our guests?

I started bouncing the big Thanksgiving dinner idea around the school, but some other teachers weren't quite as receptive as I would've hoped: "You are going to do what? Are you crazy?"

But some people did decide to join in on the ground level. The history teacher offered to teach the background of Thanksgiving and create the decorations. The math teacher decided to deal with recipes and measurements for the feast. The P.E. teachers would utilize their skills to show the students some of the games that had been played at the time of the Pilgrims. Now that the educational part of the day was sorted out, it was time to get the grub.

I wrote to local businesses and grocery stores, asking for support. I also solicited help from San Diego State University students. Several grocers agreed to sell me 30 turkeys at cost, and to donate other fixings. The children and I went shopping. Have you ever taken 40 kids who speak limited English into a supermarket to pick food for over 200 people?

The kids' eyes were wide in amazement as they ogled the won-

RAINBOW

My heart leaps up when I behold

A rainbow in the sky:

So was it when my life began;

So is it now I am a man;

So be it when I shall grow old,

Or let me die!

The Child is father of the Man;

And I could wish my day to be

Bound each to each by natural piety.

—William Wordsworth

derful array of traditional Thanksgiving foods.

The real work lay before me when I got all the food home. I can now report that I peeled 70 pounds of potatoes, prepared 20 celery relish plates and baked 20 pumpkin pies.

But there was no way I was going to be able to roast all those turkeys.

The turkey-cooking problem loomed large in my mind as the principal and school secretaries dropped into my classroom to hear us practicing our Thanksgiving song, "We Are One; We Are the United States of America."

Soon, others teachers began stopping by, offering to cook a few turkeys in their ovens. Other staffers also volunteered, as did some parents and college-student volunteers. One college guy took a turkey back to his dorm to roast after confessing he'd never cooked *anything* before. When he brought back a handsome, browned bird, he told me he'd met several cute girls while seeking cooking lessons. I was left with only three turkeys to roast—a number I could manage.

An unexpected blessing came from a former schoolmate of mine, Tara Slatton, who owned a catering business. A couple of days before our dinner, she evaluated the logistics of the situation and announced, "Okay, Miss O, I will bring the trailer and the hot steam tables and we'll set up on the morning of the event!" Tara came not only with the tables but with helpers, candied yams, drinks, and fresh-baked mince pies.

And my students? Well, they were the brilliantly gracious hosts of the luncheon. In broken English, they greeted every guest and asked each adult which Thanksgiving foods they liked the most. They sang their song and received a standing ovation.

My students and I agreed that the event had been a great success. It unified us and, even with all the work it involved, we'd had fun. As my best English speaker commented of the class, "We are the immigrants of today, but we are the citizens of tomorrow."

Maryann Ostermeyer continues to teach at the Cajon Valley Middle School.

CHRISTMAS ROSE
Rusty Fischer

I had no one to pick up at the airport that desolate Christmas Eve, but if I had to sit in my one-bedroom apartment and stare at my little Charlie Brown Christmas tree blinking on and off for even one second more, I might do myself in. I needed to go somewhere where there would be people. I just wanted to make contact with someone.

It was all I wanted for Christmas—someone to tell me that there was something in life to which I could look forward.

So I got dressed, trying to imagine what I *would* wear if I *did* have someone to meet at an arrival gate. I drove to the airport slowly, feeling the silent flickers of hope dance around my lonely heart. Maybe I'd take a seat next to another hopeful, lonely soul, and strike up a holiday conversation about something inane, like the origins of mistletoe. Who knows? With so many people streaming in for the holidays, there was even a chance that I could run into an old friend, returning home, and we'd talk for a few minutes about old times.

When I finally got to the airport, I put quarters into the parking meter, literally buying me time to fulfill my hope.

The terminal was crowded that night. But that was what I was there for, to be around people. It was after 11, and holiday travelers were rushing to and fro. I watched them hurry to get to their gates, anxious to catch their late-night flights so that they could wake up at home on Christmas morning. I began to feel out of place without a carry-on bag or a rolling piece of sleek, black luggage filled with corny last-minute gifts like Santa Claus boxer shorts.

I worried for an instant that someone might find me out. Discover that I wasn't really traveling anywhere. But the moment

quickly passed. People seemed too wrapped up in their schedules. Those traveling in clusters—were they families?—appeared
flustered and mean. People in these little groups were scowling
and arguing over who would carry what bag. Holiday tension
seemed at its height, and not only in my head. I watched a young
couple fight in the gift shop because he'd bought a shiny new
paperback she said they couldn't afford.

I found a snack bar and bought a petrified hotdog, greasy fries
and a runny chocolate milkshake. I knew I should lose some
weight, but it was a small Christmas gift to myself. Besides, eat-
ing was something to do.

I went to clean some mustard off my sweater, but then stopped
myself. Maybe if someone noticed it, that someone would actually pay attention to me. I wandered around the ticket counters
and shoeshine stands for a while, waiting for someone to speak
up. Or just nod at me as he or she went about his or her business. But no one did.

Carols blared from the speakers above me. Women, clinging to
bulging shopping bags, sighed loudly as a signal for me to move
out of their way. One elderly lady pushed me aside with an elbow
that was surprisingly strong. A man in a well-tailored suit
stepped on my toes. Two punks pointed at my sweater and
laughed. An attractive flight attendant in a tight uniform rolled
her eyes when she caught me looking at her.

I made my way to a Delta gate waiting area and took a vacant
seat. An old woman across from me dabbed at her nose with a
tissue. She looked worn out, and she was staring into space. I
wrote a story for her in my mind: of spoiled children who never
called and grandchildren who wouldn't recognize her if they
passed on the street. But could that be right?

I was rising to approach her when a large, happy family, boom-
ing with the announcement that they'd found some cold medi-

cine, swallowed her into their midst. Her smile made the Christmas lights seem dim.

I should have been happy for her.

I picked at the crusty glob of mustard on my sweater and wondered what was the point of living? I let my depression roll my imagination in morbid directions.

A crinkling of plastic broke through my black thoughts. I looked around to find its source. A single red rose surrounded by baby's breath and wrapped in dime-store plastic crackled nearby in a pale hand.

The young man—more boy than man really—holding the rose walked toward the gate. He appeared to be freshly showered, with still-wet hair slicked back. His large hands fumbled with, then smoothed, the noisy wrap around his frail flower. The rose had to be for someone very special to him.

I turned to the oversized window in time to see a plane pulling up to the gate. I stood up as if I, too, had someone to greet. Soon, the disembarked passengers surged toward the expectant crowd. Several new arrivals rushed into waiting arms, then strolled with their relative or friend toward the baggage pick-up area. I heard dozens of people say "Merry Christmas" or exchange other greetings. A glance at the clock showed that midnight had passed: Christmas Day was here.

Soon, only the fresh-faced boy and myself were left. I hung back so he wouldn't think I was stalking him, although in a way I was.

A last, deplaned passenger emerged into the terminal. She was no beauty but, as soon as she saw the young man, her smile turned her into one. He gave her the flower; she took it gently before hugging him for a quick but intense moment. As they walked away, whispering to each other, I saw her glance at the lovely rose.

Many things have happened in my life since that very early morning when a pair of innocent strangers showed me that love is worth wading through life for. A slender moment, you say, and that's true, but it was all the sign I needed that happiness was something that might come to me. It was enough to make me slough off my despair. It was a holiday miracle.

No matter how hectic or wild things get in my holiday season, I never forget to buy a single red rose on Christmas Eve. And being handed that rose is one of my beautiful wife's favorite holiday traditions.

Rusty Fischer is the author of The 25 Stories of Christmas (*www.xlibris.com/25StoriesofChristmas*.html) *and the editor of the Virtue Victorious volume,* FAITH: True Stories of Friendship, Principle and Belief. *He lives in Orlando, Florida.*

A CHILD'S CHRISTMAS IN JAIL
Tekla Dennison Miller

Gate One slammed shut. It shook the small room, which held six speechless children. Each child surrendered to a tall man in a gray uniform for a search. Once searched, they lined up against Gate Two.

I was the warden of Huron Valley Women's Prison in Michigan. I watched Kyle, a four-year old, cower in the corner farthest from where the line formed. He cried when it was his turn to be searched. Officer Johnson squatted and faced Kyle. "What's the problem, my man?"

Kyle wiped his right arm across his nose, leaving a line of mucus on his cheek.

"Let's blow your nose and talk." Johnson took a tissue from a box on a stainless steel table bolted to the cinder-block wall.

Kyle's tears formed tiny lines in his serious, man-like face.

"Your mama's waiting for you." Officer Johnson wrapped his arm around Kyle's shoulder and nodded toward Gate Two. "You know what else?"

Kyle's lower lip quivered when he shook his head no. He wiped his nose again with his arm while holding the tissue in the other hand.

"We're going to party."

The waiting children cheered. "I have to be searched now," Kyle said. Straightening, he looked quite handsome, although his dress shirt was too big for him.

Kyle held out his arms. Johnson patted him down and called out, "Gate Two!"

The children clasped their hands over their ears when the clanking gate slid open. Officer Johnson stepped through the gate first, motioned the children to follow and shouted, "Let's party!"

As Gate Two banged closed, the children formed a line behind the officer and marched like toy soldiers to the visiting room. I followed as they advanced, tugging at their unfamiliar dress clothes.

None of the children seemed to notice the officer observing them from a tiny room—the bubble, built with bulletproof glass from waist-high to the ceiling.

Kyle lagged behind and stood on tiptoe, peering through the windows of a nearby office door as though looking for something or someone he recognized.

When they reached the visiting center, Officer Johnson pulled open the steel door. He ushered the single file of "little people," as he called them, into the room decorated for Christmas. He chuckled as their faces lit up when they spotted the huge pile of wrapped presents under the tree. Their shouts mixed with the chatter and laughter of other children already in the room with the women inmates. That day, the inmates were allowed make-up and street clothes.

The new children rushed the tree—all but Kyle. He took slow, deliberate steps. When he reached the tree, he studied every branch, from the base to the angel at the top. Officer Johnson leaned toward me and said, "I remember the first time I had to search children." He shook his head. "I couldn't imagine why. They aren't the criminals."

But as both Johnson and I knew, during that first search day he'd found a syringe tucked inside the diaper of a three-month-old. Kyle had been the baby in that diaper—he was being used as a mule to ferry drugs to his mother, Janine. She'd been charged with a new felony and placed on non-contact visits. Janine's friend, Lola, who was the person who'd brought Kyle for the visit, later went to jail.

Janine had been sentenced to prison for armed robbery on her 18th birthday. She'd never taken responsibility for her offense,

claiming, "I had no choice. I couldn't get work and I needed food." Janine also never confessed that the stolen money was for Billy, her crack-addict boyfriend, who had forced her into prostitution to pay for his habit. He'd found her on the street—a vulnerable 15-year-old runaway. She'd believed Billy loved her. He also got her pregnant.

Rushed to the hospital only two days after her sentencing, Janine delivered Kyle. He weighed only four pounds and suffered from crack addiction. Janine once had told me, "I think prison is a blessing. I'm not hustling to the ER with broken arms, ribs and nose." Touching her nose, she'd added, "Billy didn't tolerate any excuses."

Billy never bothered to visit Janine.

For four years, Janine had watched Kyle grow up through the scratched plexi-glass of the non-contact booth. I'd decided that Christmas was the right time for Janine to have a real visit with her son.

Janine stood alone in the farthest corner of the room and never took her eyes off Kyle as he explored the tree. He poked his fingers into the piled gifts, his eyes widening with wonder, and I saw Janine wipe away a tear.

Prison employees had donated the tree and decorations. Today, the beige-on-beige visiting room was aglow in a hodge-podge of color. The inmates had made colored paper chains and hung them on the bare walls. Even the brown plastic stacking chairs seemed festive, positioned next to card tables covered in poinsettia-patterned paper cloths, with huge red plastic bowls filled with candy canes as centerpieces.

The night before, prisoner moms had gathered in the gym to wrap gifts donated by the Salvation Army. As they'd covered each toy with gold paper and red and green ribbon, they'd sung carols and talked about the Christmas trees they hoped to have one day in living rooms of their own.

Watching Kyle, I wondered if he understood all he'd seen: the gun tower, the 12-foot fence topped with razor ribbon.

Kyle's eyes darted from one adult face to another, probably searching for a woman who resembled the one he visited every week. When he'd been younger, a social worker had held him against the window of the visitor's booth so that he might see the stranger's face on the other side—the face of the woman the social worker had said was his mother. At four, Kyle was able to lift himself onto the steel table to reach the wall phone. Pressing his face against the window to see his mother's face better, he'd trace her image on the plastic while they talked over the telephone.

"We never talk about prison or Billy," Janine had told me not long before. "And Kyle never calls me Mommy. He never calls me anything."

Janine approached me. "Thank you, Warden Miller, for letting me off non-contact status," she said, and formed a weak smile.

"You deserve it, Janine," I answered. "Why don't you go to Kyle? I think he's looking for you."

"What will I do if he won't talk to me or let me touch him?" Janine asked. She remained motionless. She chewed her lower lip and sagged against the wall.

I touched her shoulder. "The first time is always the hardest. This will get easier with each visit."

Kyle was smaller than other boys his age. Janine and I had often talked about reports that noted that he was developmentally behind, seemed emotionally troubled and hardly talked. Janine had said, "I hope that these visits will change all that. I dream of the day when the social worker tells me Kyle's stopped fighting with the neighborhood kids."

Now Janine sighed and said, "Might as well get this over."

When she reached Kyle, Janine called out his name and touched his small arm. Kyle yanked it away and spun around. He looked like a startled fawn on the side of the road, caught in headlights.

"Don't *you* remember me?" Janine asked, choking out the words. She smiled but her chin quivered.

Kyle's affirmative nod was slow. "You look bigger than the one in the window," he commented.

Then silence, as they faced each other.

I moved in. "How about some punch and cookies?" I offered. "Santa Claus is due to arrive any minute, and we want to be ready, don't we?"

For the second time that day, and perhaps in years, Kyle's smile changed his little man's pensive face into that of a four-year-old.

"Thanks, Warden Miller," Janine said, and handed a plate of cookies to Kyle.

I whispered, "You can do this, Janine."

Kyle devoured his cookies and chugged the punch. Janine grinned at him.

The prison counselor had told me that the children in the special visitation program suffered less depression and anxiety than those who only saw their mothers through the plexiglass, or in relatively private visits. Each child felt better about his or her mother, knowing that she was not the only mom in prison. One positive result was that when the child went home he was less likely to fight, "defending" his mom's reputation.

After Janine handed another cookie to Kyle, she said to me, "I hope I have the patience. Not like before when I had to have everything right now." She snickered. "That's how I got here."

"HO! HO! HO!" Santa Claus arrived, carrying a large sack over her shoulder. Latisia, a six-foot lifer, was playing the role in a donated Santa suit, and red and green striped socks that covered the area between the bottom of the pants and her state-issued, black rubber prison boots.

Kyle and the other kids ran to Santa. Latisia pressed her way to "Santa's chair," placed to the right of the tree. Then she called out each child's name and handed him or her a gift. They seized their presents with candy-cane-sticky fingers. When Kyle heard his name, he looked at Janine. She nodded. He stepped toward Santa, hands outstretched.

The opening of presents was accompanied by joyous shrills. Within minutes, the visiting room was covered with a blizzard of torn wrapping paper and ribbons. Children jumped into the piles. The room was a happy place.

The joy was broken by the announcement that came over the P.A. system: Visiting hours are over.

Mothers and children froze in place and stared at the wall speaker. After one mother hugged her child goodbye, the others followed. Lucy, a three-year old, tugged at her mother, begging to stay. An officer forced them apart and led the teary Lucy away.

Janine reached her arms out toward Kyle but retracted them. Perhaps she feared he would recoil. Then Kyle gave her a quick hug and, clutching his new yellow plastic dump truck, skipped to the door. He stopped and turned. Janine called out, "See ya next week," and gave him a little wave good-bye. She was rewarded by Kyle's very special smile.

Tekla Dennison Miller is co-editor of the Virtue Victorious volume, JUSTICE: True Stories of Fair Play. *She is now a criminal-justice system consultant and the author of a memoir,* A Bowl of Cherries *(publishamerica.com).*

A THOUSAND CRANES
Jill Delsigne

I didn't bother to look out the window at the desert when we reached Arizona. On the long drive south from Montana, we'd passed much I'd never seen before, but I'd ignored most of it. I was 11 years old, and intent on harnessing the power of a thousand paper cranes—cranes connected to hope, according to ancient Japanese legend.

I'd created so many origami cranes that, during the previous night, folds of paper had occupied my dreams.

The first hundred cranes had been painful. Anxiety about my sick grandfather, whom we were going to visit, had made my fingers thick and awkward. Now, the constant folding had become a type of meditation. But still, I worried. I wanted to finish a thousand cranes, because the Japanese believe that a thousand cranes give power to a wish, and I needed that power with me for my grandfather. But I wasn't sure I'd finish a thousand before Christmas Eve.

My family and I arrived in Yuma too soon. I still had two hundred more cranes to make, but we could not delay the visit to grandfather. The nurses had decorated the hospital using "Jingle Bells" wrapping paper to transform each patient's door into a Christmas present. As the door swung open, I gasped. My grandfather was so small, compared to the giant he had been. The cancer had eaten his powerful muscles, but at least it hadn't taken his welcoming smile.

Grandpa said to me, "Punky, there's a place on the door where it doesn't say Jingle Bells."

I can't say I was surprised to be greeted with a puzzle. Grandpa had always given me things to think about.

Soon, a nurse shooed us from the hospital, and so we went to

his empty house. There, I folded more cranes. It was calming.

Relatives trickled into the house throughout the day. Some relatives hadn't seen me for five years. They fondly and loudly greeted one another, and me. I heard, "Look how *big* you've gotten!" again and again. I didn't feel big; I felt very small. And I wondered why the relatives didn't sound sadder—they *knew* what was going on behind the hospital Christmas door. But I figured maybe grown-ups just talk a lot when they're worried.

The next day, my immediate family visited my grandfather again. He caught my eyes searching the door. "Did you find *it* yet, Dolly?" he asked.

I shook my head solemnly, but his eyes twinkled in return. I wanted desperately to see what he saw.

On Christmas Eve, we returned to the hospital to bring Grandpa home. My older brother effortlessly picked him up. This was painful for me to witness. How could God have made my strong grandfather so light? I touched the origami paper in my pocket to hold back my tears.

My relatives still filled the house with unnatural, forced noise. Everyone unwrapped presents and took pictures. What kept me calm was not the synthetic cheer but the knowledge that I had finally finished the thousand paper birds. They filled a large box. Most were made from smooth, colorful origami paper. Some I had made from candy wrappers.

I proudly presented my grandfather with the cranes. Faltering, I explained about the Japanese legend, and how I wanted to give him a wish. With a sad smile, he whispered, "Thanks, Punky."

It didn't occur to me then that my grandfather might be ready to die, that his wish might be to end his pain. It wasn't an idea I was old enough to consider. My thought, with every paper crane I'd made, was that I was creating a way to keep my grandfather alive.

Christmas is the most hopeful holiday, in my view. Christmas infuses a season of long, dark nights with the remembrance of the birth of the child capable of redeeming the world from its sins.

My grandfather died after Christmas, leaving me with *two* riddles to solve.

I hadn't seen what my grandfather had found so significant on the hospital door. Now, I suspect that the secret message was that he wanted me to look at the cheerful door and not into his pain. He directed me into a lighthearted game so I might escape my own sorrow.

The second riddle was: Could a thousand cranes mean one thing to me, and the opposite to my grandfather?

Now, I can acknowledge that probably they did.

I am certain, though, that the cranes pulled me through that Christmas and my grandfather's death. And I fully realize that in the face of pain and dying, humanity depends upon hope to continue living.

I know now that a thousand cranes are neither a hope for life or for death. A thousand cranes carry with them no specific objective; they simply and profoundly symbolize hope itself.

Jill Delsigne of Clancy, Montana, is a junior at Scripps College in Claremont, California.

SECTION VII

♦ PASSING THE TORCH ♦

*"Life is no brief candle to me; it is sort of a splendid torch which
I have got hold of for a moment, and I want to make it burn as brightly as possible before handing it on to future generations."*
—GEORGE BERNARD SHAW

THE BIG TEST

Gary Anderson

When my kids were very young, I made a vow not to be one of those parents who lived their lives vicariously through the accomplishments of their children. And I did fairly well, too, until my first child, my daughter, Casey Rose, entered kindergarten.

I began to keep a running total of every smiley-face and happy-bunny sticker she earned—the equivalent of an "A"—which was as good as it could get at her school.

Who knows? I found myself wondering. We just might have a future Nobel Prize winner in our household! After all, I doubted that even Albert Einstein brought home straight smiley faces when he was Casey Rose's age, and look where he ended up. As I watched my daughter's progress I was filled with pride.

Then one day, Casey Rose got off the school bus and came running up the driveway, holding out a sheet of paper. Since she usually kept her school papers in her backpack, I knew this was something special. She stuffed the paper into my hand and I read it as we walked, hand-in-hand, back to the house.

The paper read, "In two weeks, we will be doing some special testing at the school. Please make certain your child gets a good night's rest the night before."

Whoa! I thought. *Special testing.* That sounded serious.

Against my better judgment, I began to worry about how my daughter would do. This was to be her first big test, and there'd been no instructions on how I could help her prepare for it. The whole concept made me nervous, so I decided to have a chat with her teacher.

The next day, I drove to the school to pick up Casey Rose. Her teacher, Mrs. Kurth, was standing in front of the school, and I asked if she had time to talk awhile. She said she'd be delighted, and led us back to her classroom.

Once in the room, Mrs. Kurth, a short, portly lady with a sweet expression and a gentle voice, asked me to have a seat. Looking around, I saw nothing but miniature chairs and tables, but I finally managed to settle myself down onto a doll-sized chair (no mean feat for a guy 6' 2") and we began to talk. I poured out my concerns about the fact that Casey Rose had never taken a test before, and how the note the school had sent home had made me feel as if this was going to be something serious.

Mrs. Kurth just sat quietly, smiling demurely, waiting for me to finish. It occurred to me that she'd been through all this before. Finally, I asked, "What can I do to help Casey Rose prepare for this big day?"

Without a moment's hesitation, Mrs. Kurth said, "Give her a hug."

Although she'd said it softly, her words hit me like a thunderbolt. I was stunned, but also humbled. In an instant, I realized that I *had* been making too much of a simple kindergarten test. And I'd almost violated the vow I'd made so long ago *not* to push my kids too hard. I smiled, made my way to my feet, thanked Mrs. Kurth and scooped my daughter into my arms.

Many years have gone by since that day in Mrs. Kurth's classroom, and Casey Rose has faced many challenges since that first big test. But through the years, every time I've watched my daughter approach one of those life tests I know we all must face, her kindergarten teacher's words have come back to me, and I've remembered that the best thing I can do for my child is simply to give her a hug.

Gary Anderson of Elgin, Iowa, is a columnist for the magazine, Iowa REC News, *and the author of* Spider's Big Catch *(Writers Club Press).*

TRACKS IN THE BLACKBOARD JUNGLE
Amy Verner

I was 28 when I decided to be a teacher, and for a time I thought that I could change the world. I believed that by helping to educate troubled inner city youth, I might help them rise above their circumstances and give them a chance at productive, happy lives.

Aware of the political rhetoric about how schools are failing today's poorer students, I assumed my good will could make a difference when I went to work in a tough school in the south Seattle metro area. I wouldn't merely be there for a paycheck; I'd be in the classroom for the students, to really help them learn.

As a 9th grade English teacher, I also hoped that exposing teens to literature would help them envision a different kind of life for themselves. I thought they'd recognize the yearning and passionate heat of the young lovers in *Romeo and Juliet.* And perhaps some students could relate the lesson of the feud between the Capulets and Montagues to street feuds today, and see how futile gang rivalry is. I even imagined that a few students might glimpse Shakespeare as the supreme rapper of his time, and of all time. Above all, I wanted my students to sense that there was a timeless world of poetry and theater that could portray real problems and that might spur their own imaginations.

Things didn't go as I'd hoped. Some kids lacked the reading and vocabulary skills to understand the play's simplest lyrics. Others might be up to it, but could not admit that it might warrant their time. How could I make the romantic poetry of *Romeo and Juliet* relevant to kids busy dealing with their hard-knock lives?

The overwhelming poverty and violence of the neighborhood walked through the school doors every morning, in the form of middle-school drug addicts, gang members and prostitutes.

> *"The grand essentials of happiness are: something to do,*
> *something to love, and something to hope for."*
> —ALLAN K. CHALMERS

Good kids had to be on guard and maintain "attitude" in front of more hardened classmates, while also watching their backs and maintaining their spirits at home.

A lone school-based family advocate—there'd been two before budget cuts—worked fulltime to keep kids' family problems at bay so that they could get on with the business of learning. Even in the best of families, wrenching poverty beat down on the kids. It is hard to do homework when you're homeless and have to stand in line at the food bank for dinner.

I understood *why* these kids—filled with pain in their lives and adult examples of rage—would lash out in school, but that didn't mean I could weather the consequences with equanimity. At one time or another during my first years of teaching, students threatened me with fists, knives or guns.

Enormously upsetting were the letters I received from students, detailing their plans for suicide. I would follow the proper channels so that the counselors on staff could help them, but it saddened me that these children thought of suicide as the answer to their problems.

I began my sixth year of teaching, wondering why I'd come back. I no longer believed I could make a difference. The previous term had ended with the news that a student, with whom I'd been working, and who I thought was making progress, had been arrested for a brutal stabbing right outside of the school grounds.

The memory of that student weighted me down as I staggered up two flights of crumbling concrete stairs to my classroom early on the first morning. The stairwells and corridors were dim, thanks to the shattered light fixtures that had not been replaced over the summer. I was listening for footsteps behind me and was relieved when I heard none. I hated getting to school early because of this lonely darkness. No security guards were in sight.

Reaching my room and unlocking the door, I realized I'd been holding my breath. I didn't let it out again until I had closed the door behind me and locked out possible intruders.

"Good morning!" The loud, deep and Spanish-accented voice startled me, and it took me a minute to remember that this year I'd be sharing a room with one of our math teachers because there weren't enough classrooms to go around.

"Uh, good morning," I replied. "How are you this morning, Mr. Mendoza?"

The math teacher had a shaved head and a nasty looking scar on this throat. I didn't know the history of the scar but I knew of Mr. Mendoza's charisma. Students and staff alike were drawn to him. Mr. Mendoza answered my automatic question: "I am wonderful today! I am thrilled to be here in this place in this time! How are you?"

I blurted out the truth: "Well, if you really want to know, I am sick and tired of being a psychiatrist, parent, triage nurse, drug counselor, friend, anger-management counselor and hand-holder for these awful kids." My pulse was racing and I could hold nothing back. "I am even more tired of being a whipping boy for parents who can't seem to find the resources to raise their own children, and expect me to do it for them!"

I looked around our shabby classroom, whose newest piece of equipment was a 20-year-old personal computer. "I have to teach with books that the kids can't take home because there aren't enough to go around. Most of this year's students won't be able to read or write. Nothing I can do makes the slightest bit of difference—for them or for me. I can't sleep at night worrying that

Jenny is on the streets again or Kyle is getting jumped into his brother's gang. Will Darnel come to school again covered with bruises? And how many won't show up because they're in jail? And belong there! I'm sick of this. I can't do it any more."

Mr. Mendoza gazed at me after I finished speaking. He let the silence settle between us, and then he quietly asked, "Did you know that I am from a very bad part of Los Angeles?"

I shook my head no, and he continued. His neighborhood, he said, had been prime street gang turf. He told me that he'd been one of six kids. His father was serving a life sentence for murder; his mother was often overwhelmed. His story seemed no different than many of our students' stories; I felt impatient with it. Knowing the kids would soon be in, I started to move around the room. The first thing I had to do was lock up my purse so it wouldn't get stolen.

Mr. Mendoza went on with his story. He said that although his mother had warned him against the gangs, he had found them enticing. One day, when he was 12, he drove the getaway car for his brother's gang as they staged a retaliatory raid on rivals who'd stolen their drugs. That night, his house was targeted. His brother, who'd been smoking a cigarette on the porch, was killed by gunshot, and another bullet pierced a wall and wounded his baby sister.

His personal history had my attention now. How had my colleague survived all this?

The shootings, he admitted, had not *changed* him. They'd simply focused him on revenge. The follow week, he and another brother and their friends went looking for their attackers but ended up ambushed by them. His second brother was killed; Mendoza's throat was cut, and he was left for dead.

Now, I understood the scar.

The police found Mendoza. He was taken to the hospital. His

life was saved. But he also had to face juvenile court, and not for the first time. He was paroled but placed in a school in a new district where he was unknown.

He was pointed on the road to change, he said, by an English teacher who had the class read *The Outsiders* by S. E. Hinton. In this contemporary story of how a gang member struggles to redefine himself after witnessing a violent murder, Mendoza was amazed to find characters to whom he could relate. The teacher asked students to write about the book. Mendoza poured out his own story in his paper.

Writing down his story made him see he didn't want to live it any longer. Mendoza's teacher became his champion.

I stared at Mr. Mendoza. A book and a teacher changed his life? It was possible?

The math teacher was not finished. Looking in the mirror each morning, Mendoza was reminded by his scar of the life he'd escaped. He also remembered his English schoolteacher who didn't confuse his hoodlum exterior for the possibilities inside him. Mr. Mendoza reminded me that I didn't necessarily know the whole story about my students. Another thing I could not know was how something I did or said could affect them down the road. He advised me to "let go" of the negatives in students' lives that I couldn't control, and concentrate on teaching as well as I could.

I went through my first day of school routines, feeling somewhat better. A banquet was scheduled for that evening to celebrate students who'd overcome failing records to be promoted on schedule. But I thought I'd better skip it to think over what Mr. Mendoza had said, and to get a jumpstart on lesson plans. I was packing up for the day when a former pupil, who was a recovering drug addict, asked me if I'd be at the dinner. I realized that her parents would not be there. It was suddenly clear that I should be. That's what Mr. Mendoza's English teacher would have done.

At the banquet, my student hugged me and thanked me and made me promise to come to her high school graduation. I knew I'd be there.

The next morning, when someone asked me how I was doing, without thinking I replied, "Great! Thrilled to be here!"

And, eight years later, I still am.

The "Mr. Mendoza" in this essay is an amalgam of two colleagues who inspired Amy Verner to keep teaching. Ms. Verner was recently nominated for Seattle's Teacher of the Year Award.

HEAVEN-SENT

Kate Vega

I kept having an impossible dream, a really impossible dream, during my pregnancy. The dream was that my grandmother was helping me get ready for the birth of my child.

But the grandmother I'd so loved had died three years earlier.

I'd been unhappily married before she died, although I'd never told her so. But I think she'd sensed it if only because this woman who loved babies had never asked me about my own plans in that area.

It was not until after my grandmother had gone that I'd divorced, and then met and married Pedro, who is my true love. Now Pedro and I were expecting a child, and my grandmother kept reappearing in both my dreams and reveries.

It made a funny kind of sense, though, because my grandmother had been a pediatric nurse. She used to tell me stories of how she loved to make "snooky curls" on babies with lots of hair. After she retired, she volunteered on the newborn ward at the hospital.

She liked all babies, but the great-grandchild in my belly would have been very special to her.

My cousin, Kristin, who had inherited my grandmother's knitting needles and crochet hooks, told me she'd make an afghan for my new baby, just as our grandmother had made afghans for us when we were born. I was touched by Kristin's plan, yet I took it as another sad reminder that no way could my grandmother truly greet my child.

The next week, Pedro and I drove 12 hours to New Jersey for a baby shower in my honor. I should have been happy, but the ride had been hard on me and I was still thinking about my grandmother. I didn't understand why I couldn't shake my melancholy. The night before the shower, I prayed, asking God to soothe my troubled mind. I also made a request unlike any I'd made before. I asked Him to send me a sign if my grandmother really was watching over me. I fell asleep, feeling foolish.

The next morning, I awoke with no memory of the night's dreams. I summoned my energy to get ready for the shower, which was going to be a big affair.

As the house filled up with people later that day, my Aunt Judy pulled me into another room, where Pedro, my grandfather and father were sharing a couch. Aunt Judy, who had been my grandmother's youngest and favorite child, said she had something she wanted to do before the party officially started. She produced a gift bag. "It's from Grandma," she said with tears in her eyes.

I peered inside the bag and also began to cry, pulling out a snowy-white baby afghan, just like the ones my grandmother had made for every newborn. The men in my family jumped up from the couch to hug me.

Aunt Judy told us how a few months before she died, my grandmother had gotten it into her head that she had to go to the craft store to pick out yarn for the afghan she needed to make for "Kate's baby." When my aunt had remarked that a child didn't seem part of my near future, my grandmother had insisted that it was time for her to get started on the afghan.

I touched the afghan to my face; I could smell the faint odor of my grandmother's perfume.

Soon after my baby was born I wrapped him in this white blanket of love. When he is older, I will tell him about his great-grandmother watching over us.

Kate Vega lives in Columbia, South Carolina, with her husband and their son, Salvador.

A REAL FATHER
Jane Jaffe Young

When Paul Graham faced the breakdown of his 18-year marriage in 1983, he asked himself: What would happen to his relationship with his three children if he and his wife divorced? Thinking about it, Paul came to the conclusion that it could only improve. Not only might their children be able to grow up in a less tense atmosphere, he and his wife, independently, might actually have *more* good times with the children.

As it was, both he and his wife, Helene, had hectic career schedules, and so did their over-scheduled kids: fourteen-year-old John and the eight-year-old twins, Katherine and Nicholas. The way things had gone, nobody had much incentive to stay home. But once he and his wife parted, surely there'd be a custodial and visiting arrangement that assured each of them time with the children they both loved. Paul looked forward to re-establishing the kind of close and playful relationship he'd had with his kids when they were younger.

Although I'd been Paul's colleague for 16 years, I hadn't really known him when he was married and living in suburbia. At the time he left his wife, I was 43 years old, divorced and living in Manhattan with my 13-year-old daughter, Victoria. It was then I became his confidante. My own divorce had been an amicable one. My husband and I had shared a matrimonial lawyer, and Victoria spent time with each of us.

The emotional hell Paul described to me was *terra incognita*. From the day he'd left his home, he'd become the devil incarnate. When his wife had heard he was leaving, she warned him that she'd cut him out of their children's lives, and she was making good on that threat.

Within days of Paul's departure, he'd started receiving screaming phone calls from the kids, at all hours of the day and night. Soon, his wife apparently armed one child with a sheaf of bills— bills not mentioned before to Paul—and had sent the poor child into Paul's workplace to confront him publicly with his alleged lack of support.

In the midst of this distressing assault by pint-sized "avengers," Helene agreed to let Paul visit the children. The boys sat silent, arms folded, stiff and stony-faced. Only Katherine was her usual giggling, affectionate self. When Paul returned a week later, Helene would not leave him alone with the children, so he left, the twins shouting after him, "We don't ever want to see you again!"

Walking to the railroad station, he was served an order of protection accusing him of having physically abused the children on his previous visit and of "exposing himself" to his daughter. His lawyer advised him never again to visit his children without a witness.

Paul's distress was palpable to all who knew him. The worst part was his worry that his children genuinely hated him. Even after he'd learned about "the parental alienation syndrome," where children caught up in divorce become pathologically over-identified with the custodial parent and act out against their other parent, he vowed not to give up. He *loved* John, Katherine and Nicholas, and there had to be a way he could have a normal, loving relationship with them.

He met all his financial obligations to his family promptly, even paying extras, so his wife could not make money a cause of complaint. He denied himself many small things—luxuries were out of the question. He sent his children gifts, which were unacknowledged or returned.

Paul was continually served with new complaints and summonses, including one charging that he made obscene, insulting phone calls to his oldest son. Nothing could have been further from the truth, yet John testified against his father at a hearing, and the judge forbade Paul to contact his wife or children.

That, however, did not prevent *them* from phoning him. He told me about one particularly devastating call from the twins, in which he thought they'd been reading from some sort of script. As Paul recounted it, one twin said: "You're playing a terrible game to see if we'll starve to death by taking away more and more money. You can't be our *real* father. A *real* father would never do the horrible things you've done. A *real* father would make sure the mommy and children would have everything they need and are happy all the time."

Paul was sure of what his child had said because, following his lawyer's advice, he was taping such calls and recording the words in a journal he was keeping.

Meanwhile, Paul went on paying child support of $21,000 a year—no small sum for a college professor. His children were talented, and sometimes sang or danced in large public performances. Paul did the sleuthing necessary to figure out when one of his children might be seen—then watched him or her through binoculars from a back-row seat. He was not allowed to hug the child afterwards. It was heartbreaking. I know, because by this time Paul and I had become more than just friends, and I once accompanied him.

Eighteen months after he'd separated from Helene, a new lawyer "won" him official visitation at 3 PM on Fridays. Off he'd go—a one-hour train trip to Westchester, a three-mile walk from the station—and arrive at the house only to discover it seemingly empty. Every so often, though, the door would suddenly be flung open, and the twins would appear, shrieking, "Get off our property! You should be in jail!"

For over a year and a half, Paul made these fruitless treks, refusing to admit the situation would not change. Finally, he heeded the advice of a psychiatrist specializing in custody and divorce, and temporarily gave up. "Stay in touch with them over the years through cards and presents," the doctor had advised. "Let them know you're available to them. It's all you can do."

His older son graduated high school and was admitted to an Ivy League college. Paul knew because he received notices from the college. And John knew where he could find his father, but he wasn't ready to do that. When he finished college, he went on to study music at a conservatory in New York. By then, Paul's twins were 18 and in their first year at college. Paul revived his fervent hope that he'd see his children again.

Surely they were old enough now to begin to understand that not all married couples belong together. Time might have given them some insight into their mother, and given them an inkling that a father who paid all their bills, and who'd banged on their doors for so long, might actually love them.

The longed-for moment came on a fine March day in 1992 when I answered the phone and a young man asked, "Is Paul Graham there?"

"Who shall I say is calling?"

"This is John. His son."

Breathless, I almost dropped the phone in my excitement. I couldn't wait for Paul to get home and tell him the amazing news.

Later that day, father and son spoke for the first time in ten years, and agreed to meet in a neighborhood restaurant, where they spent several intense hours catching up. "He looked shell-shocked and lost," Paul told me afterwards. I learned that John's relationship with his mother had turned volatile, but he wasn't too old to still want a loving parent. At their reunion, he'd apologized to his father for shunning him for so long.

The healing began that day, although it wasn't an altogether joyful one: Paul had learned many things about how unhappy his younger children had been after he'd been banished from their lives. And yes, as we'd suspected, the twins had been given hateful scripts to rehearse before calling their dad.

Their mother had also been unable to cope with her oldest child's departure for college. For her sake, and that of his sister and brother, John had come home every other weekend, missing out on much of college life, shorting his study time and propelling himself into a breakdown.

Paul and I had many long conversations with him, and helped him in every way we could. His father was thrilled to be reconnected, and I was happy to be on the scene. John, in many ways, became my first son. We were delighted to attend openly all his performances, meet his friends and watch him transform from a lost young man into a person able to assert his own needs, interests and desires.

One year after Paul and John "found" each other, Paul's daughter, Katherine, then 19, reentered his life. She, too, was enrolled in a conservatory, but out of state. But she'd become so alarmed by certain actions of her mother that she'd fled to a friend's house, in still another state, and it was from there that she shakily telephoned her father. The healing process between father and daughter wasn't always easy, but I'm happy to say that things are good now.

When I met Paul I had one child, Victoria; now I feel I have three. Victoria and Katherine have become especially close. As a family of five, we've celebrated birthdays and some holidays. We've cried together and laughed together. John and Katherine have revealed some of their painful memories and also their hopes. We've discussed their career problems and possibilities. We all danced at Victoria's wedding. With John at the keyboard, his band played at it, too. He has toured many countries as a musician, but we can always count on his company, and his talent, at an important family event.

In a recent e-mail, Katherine observed, "One of the saddest parts of life for me is that I never had the chance to really live and grow up with Victoria, you and my dad . . . but at least I know and love you now."

There remains a hole in Paul's heart over the loss of his son (and Katherine's twin), Nicholas. Paul visited Nicholas while he was still in college but found him totally uninterested in both his father and his studies. Paul attempted to stay in touch with him, as did his sister and brother, but so far reconnection has been a lost cause. Still, we live in hope that one day that third phone call will come.

For now, though, we are grateful that Paul has been given a second chance by two of his children to be "a real father" to them.

Jane Jaffe Young, who teaches at the City University of New York, has changed some names in this essay to protect individuals' privacy. Her writing credits include articles for New York Magazine *and a book,* D.H. Lawrence on Screen.

LAYER BY LAYER

Kimberly Ripley

Have you ever tried to mail a layer cake? Yes, I said "mail" and "layer cake," too. I used to think that only a parent would consider such a feat—only a parent with a child living away from home. And only when that child's chance of success in an adult world seemed to be rapidly diminishing.

It is, in fact, a kind of art form to mail a layer cake. One precaution is that the cake must be mailed in its unfrosted state—its layers separated with sheets of wax paper and enough bubble wrap to pack a set of fine china. But before you get to that stage you must have baked the layers in foil pans, and have resolved to keep each layer safely entombed within its pan for the trip. The frosting accompanies the layers in a sealed container. In my case, I even sent a butter knife. I was relying on the talents of my son's roommate to use that knife to ice the cake. My son and his roommate had been known to be short of actual flatware.

It was my son's 19th birthday. Every year, for 18 years, Scott had been presented with one of his mother's German Chocolate layer cakes for his birthday. I was determined that number 19 would be very much like all the rest. The only problem was the 1,600 or so miles between us.

The distance was Scott's idea. Two weeks before Scott was to have graduated from high school, he had quit. He had simply walked out the door, packed his meager belongings and moved from New Hampshire to Florida.

Now, just four months later, it simply wasn't a convenient time for me to drop everything, shell out three or four hundred dollars and make a quick trip south to deliver a birthday cake. So that left one, and only one, option. The cake would have to be mailed.

Of course, while in the process of boxing this birthday cake for

The Icing on the Cake

Our family recipe for German Chocolate Cake Frosting *will generously ice three fresh-baked, cooled layers of your favorite chocolate cake. You'll want to apply the frosting between each layer as well as coat the entire cake.*

If shipping to someone, you need to send the frosting in a sealed, airtight heavy jar, protected by freezer packs, in a very cushioned box. And you must ship by guaranteed 24-hour delivery to avoid spoilage. Shipping frosting is a risky business, whose success neither I nor the publisher guarantees. My best advice, actually, is to make this frosting for a homecoming occasion.—K. R.

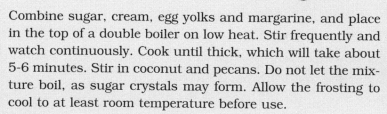

2 cups sugar

2 cups heavy cream

6 egg yolks

1 stick margarine

2 cups shredded coconut

2 cups coarsely chopped pecans

Combine sugar, cream, egg yolks and margarine, and place in the top of a double boiler on low heat. Stir frequently and watch continuously. Cook until thick, which will take about 5-6 minutes. Stir in coconut and pecans. Do not let the mixture boil, as sugar crystals may form. Allow the frosting to cool to at least room temperature before use.

its trip with the U.S. Postal Service, I came up with a few other ideas for goodies to include in the box. Mothers are famous for things like that. They think of things their kids might need and probably wouldn't buy. They think of ways (that they believe are subtle) to remind a faraway son to shower and to eat nourishing meals. They think of ways to tell a son that he is loved.

I realize now, three years later, that each of my little comfort gifts was a way of expressing my hope that Scott would not forsake the values of our family and that he would find a way to make the values his own, completing his education and working hard to achieve his goals.

I mailed lots of hope to Florida. My son opened many hope packages and laughed.

"You sent me salad dressing," he remarked during one phone call, the snicker in his voice barely detectable.

"Yes, I did. Do you like it?"

"It's great, Mom, but we never eat salads."

"Well, did you like the other things I sent?"

"Yes, Mom, and thank you. We've really had a tough time finding cans of soup and bars of soap down here."

I'm pretty sure there was sarcasm in his voice that time.

With the birthday cake, I mailed the usual celebratory items: candles, napkins, paper plates, paper cups, plastic forks, plastic spoons, plastic knives and matches to light the candles.

"You sent matches in the mail?" my husband asked, for some reason astonished that I would do such a thing.

Was there something wrong with that?

Other times I sent toothpaste and a new toothbrush, tissues, toilet paper, and trash bags, too.

Before long, the gentleman at the post office knew me by name, and knew just where the package I was carrying was headed. "What's Scott getting this time?" he'd ask.

Sometimes, I made up my answer. It might have sounded silly to tell him what was really in those packages. He might think I was babying my son. I wasn't. I was giving him encouragement.

The cake arrived completely intact. My son's roommate frosted it, added the candles and lit them with the lighter he owned. Scott told me this in his thank-you phone call.

Hmm. I guess they hadn't needed those matches after all.

As the months went by, my parcels to Scott included Halloween candy, a miniature Christmas tree, Easter eggs and boxer shorts. You know the adage about wearing clean underwear?

Scott made lots of mistakes while living away from home. It was hard for me to sit by, miles and miles away, and let him make those mistakes. However, that was part of his growing up. Scott made errors concerning his job, his money (when he had any), his health and his friendships. He made bad decisions that led to unhappy repercussions. Yet through it all, he later told me, he believed that he'd get his act together and find a road to a better life.

Scott was home for his 20th birthday. And it was a special pleasure baking the German Chocolate layer cake, knowing I need not mail it. The following April, Scott re-enrolled at his high school. On June 15, 2001, Scott proudly walked with the graduating class of Portsmouth High School and received his diploma. The principal had tears in her eyes as she hugged him. I was nearly blinded by tears of my own.

"You never gave up on me, Mom," he said on his graduation night. "And I have hope because you've always had hope."

Scott is now a painter, intent on establishing a business of his own. He remains fond of his still somewhat feckless former roommate in Florida. As his pal's birthday neared, Scott asked if I could help him with a little project. He wanted to bake a layer cake and send it to his friend. "I need you to package it for me," he said.

I was glad to show him all I knew about wrapping up hope and putting it in the mail. Have you ever mailed a layer cake? It's tricky but not impossible when you handle it with care.

Kimberly Ripley, mother of five, bakes and writes in Portsmouth, New Hampshire. She often travels to present her workshop, Freelancing Later in Life, to interested groups. For mor information, please visit www.freelancing1.homestead.com.

DAVID O. Mc
BYU-IDAHO
REXBURG ID 83460

ALSO IN THIS SERIES

COMING SOON

WISDOM: True Stories of Life's Lessons

FAITH: True Stories of Friendship, Principle & Belief

JUSTICE: True Stories of Fair Play

Visit us at www.VirtueVictorious.com to learn how you can become part of our reading and writing community.

WITHDRAWN

JUN 17 2024

DAVID O. McKAY LIBRARY
BYU-IDAHO